W9-AWS-074

THE
Little Book
of
Venom

# THE Little Book of Venom

*A Collection of Historical Insults*

COMPILED BY JENNIFER HIGGIE

CB
CONTEMPORARY BOOKS

**Library of Congress Cataloging-in-Publication Data**

[Far too noisy, my dear Mozart]
The little book of venom : a collection of historical insults / compiled by Jennifer Higgie.
p. cm.
Originally published: Far too noisy, my dear Mozart. London : M. O'Mara Books, 1997.
Includes index.
ISBN 0-8092-2808-4
1. Invective. I. Higgie, Jennifer. II. Title.
PN6231.I65F37 1998
082—dc21 98-6777
CIP

Cover illustration by Dan Krovatin

First published in Great Britain in 1997 by Michael O'Mara Books Limited, 9 Lion Yard, Tremadoc Road, London SW4 7NQ

This edition published in the United States in 1998 by
Contemporary Books
A division of NTC/Contemporary Publishing Group, Inc.
4255 West Touhy Avenue
Lincolnwood (Chicago), Illinois 60646-1975 U.S.A.

Manufactured in the United States of America
International Standard Book Number: 0-8092-2808-4
98 99 00 01 02 03 04 QP 7 6 5 4 3 2 1

# CONTENTS

THE
Little Book
of
Venom

# 1
# ON MUSIC

---

Wagner was a monster. He was anti-Semitic on Mondays and vegetarian on Tuesdays. On Wednesday he was in favor of annexing Newfoundland, Thursday he wanted to sink Venice, and Friday he wanted to blow up the pope.

*Tony Palmer, on Richard Wagner (1813–83)*

I like Wagner's music better than any other music. It is so loud that one can talk the whole time without people hearing what one says. That is a great advantage.

*Oscar Wilde (1854–1900), on Richard Wagner*

By God no, if it had been, I should have run away myself.

*The Duke of Wellington (1769–1852), replying to a question from the Russian ambassador on whether Beethoven's* Battle Symphony *was like the actual Battle of Waterloo*

Wagner, thank the fates, is no hypocrite. He says out what he means, and he usually means something nasty.

*James Gibbons Huneker, (1860–1921), American music and drama critic, on Richard Wagner*

Wagner's music is better than it sounds.

*Mark Twain (1835–1910), on Richard Wagner*

Is Wagner actually a man? Is he not rather a disease? Everything he touches falls ill: he has made music sick.

*Friedrich Wilhelm Nietzsche (1844–1900), on Richard Wagner*

Of all the bête, clumsy, blundering, boggling, baboon-blooded stuff that I ever saw on a human stage, that last night beat—as far as the story and acting went—all the affected, sapless, soulless, beginningless, endless, topless, bottomless, topsy-turviest, tuneless, scrabble-pipiest-tongs and boniest-doggerel of sounds I ever endured the deadliness of, that eternity of nothing was deadliest, as far as its sound went.

*John Ruskin (1819–1900), on Richard Wagner*

Wagner has beautiful moments but awful quarter hours.

*Gioacchino Rossini (1792–1868), on Richard Wagner*

I love Wagner, but the music I prefer is that of a cat hung up by its tail outside a window and trying to stick to the panes of glass with its claws.

*Charles Baudelaire (1821–67), on Richard Wagner*

Composition indeed! Decomposition is the proper word for such hateful fungi.

Dramatic and Musical World *(1855), on Franz Liszt (1811–86)*

He writes the ugliest music extant.

Dramatic and Musical Review *(1843), on Franz Liszt*

Liszt's bombast is bad; it is very bad; in fact there is only one thing worse in his music, and that is his affected and false simplicity. It was said of George Sand that she had a habit of speaking and writing concerning chastity in such terms that the very word became impure; so it is with the simplicity of Liszt.

*Philip Hale, Boston music critic, on Franz Liszt*

It is gaudy musical harlotry, savage and incoherent bellowings.

Boston Gazette, *on the work of Franz Liszt*

He was a fiddler and consequently a rogue.

*Jonathan Swift (1667–1745)*

Perhaps it was because Nero played the fiddle, they burned Rome.

*Oliver Herford (1863–1935)*

Berlioz composes by splashing his pen over the manuscript and leaving the issue to chance.

*Frédéric Chopin (1810–49), Polish composer, on Hector Berlioz (1803–69), French composer*

Berlioz, musically speaking, is a lunatic; a classical composer only in Paris, the great city of quacks. His music is simply and undisguisedly nonsense.

Dramatic and Musical Review *(1843)*

I can compare *Le Carnival Romain* by Berlioz to nothing but the caperings and gibberings of a big baboon, overexcited by a dose of alcoholic stimulus.

*George Templeton Strong, British critic, diary entry*

Jazz: Music invented for the torture of imbeciles.

*Henry van Dyke (1852–1933)*

It's bad when they don't perform your operas—but when they do, it's far worse.

*Camille Saint-Saëns (1835–1921), on Dame Ethel Smyth (1858–1944), composer*

Of all the bulls that live, this hath the greatest ass's ears.

> *Elizabeth I (1533–1603), on John Bull (c. 1563–1628), musician*

Far too noisy, my dear Mozart, far too many notes . . .

> *Archduke Ferdinand of Austria, on Wolfgang Amadeus Mozart (1756–91)*

After Rossini dies, who will there be to promote his music?

> *Richard Wagner, on Gioacchino Rossini*

The audience seemed rather disappointed: they expected the ocean, something big, something colossal, but they were served instead with some agitated water in a saucer.

> *Louis Schneider, music critic, on* La Mer *by Claude Debussy (1862–1918)*

I liked the bit about quarter to eleven.

> *Erik Satie (1866–1925), French composer, on "From Dawn to Noon on the Sea" from* La Mer *by Claude Debussy*

A glorified bandmaster.

*Sir Thomas Beecham (1879–1961), British conductor, on Arturo Toscanini (1867–1957), Italian conductor*

She would be like Richard Wagner if only she looked a bit more feminine.

*Osbert Sitwell (1892–1969), British poet and writer, on Dame Ethel Smyth*

A tub of pork and beer.

*Hector Berlioz, French composer, on George Frideric Handel (1685–1759), German-born British composer*

The musical equivalent of blancmange.

*Bernard Levin, British journalist, on Frederick Delius (1862–1934), British composer*

A provincial Debussy.

*A. J. P. Taylor, British historian, on Frederick Delius*

Splitting the convulsively inflated larynx of the Muse, Berg utters tortured mistuned cackling, a pandemonium of chopped-up orchestral sounds, mishandled men's throats, bestial outcries, bellowing, rattling, and all other evil noises . . . Berg is the poisoner of the well of German music.

> Germania, *on Alban Berg (1885–1935), Austrian composer*

Beethoven always sounds like the upsetting of bags—with here and there a dropped hammer.

> *John Ruskin (1819–1900), on Ludwig van Beethoven (1770–1827)*

Oh you arch-ass—you double-barreled ass!

> *Ludwig van Beethoven, on Gottfried Weber, music critic*

I liked your opera. I think I will set it to music.

> *Ludwig van Beethoven, to a fellow composer*

Shostakovich is without doubt the foremost composer of pornographic music in the history of art.

> *W. J. Henderson, music critic, on Dmitri Shostakovich (1906–75)*

. . . [I]t is impossible to deny that his music(?) is a soporific, by the side of which the telephone book is a strong cup of coffee.

*Samuel Chotzinoff, on Alban Berg (1885–1935)*

He was ignored till he began to smash the parlor furniture, throw bombs, and hitch together ten pianolas, all playing different tunes, whereupon everyone began to talk about him.

*Henry T. Fink, American music critic, on Arnold Schoenberg (1874–1951)*

A composer for one right hand.

*Richard Wagner, on Frédéric Chopin (1810–49)*

He sang like a hinge.

*Ethel Merman, on Cole Porter (1892–1964)*

Listening to the *Fifth Symphony* of Ralph Vaughan Williams is like staring at a cow for forty-five minutes.

*Aaron Copland, on Ralph Vaughan Williams (1872–1958)*

Rachmaninoff's immortalizing totality was his scowl. He was a six-and-a-half-foot scowl.

*Igor Stravinsky (1882–1971), Russian composer, on Sergey Rachmaninoff (1873–1943), Russian composer*

The musical equivalent of St. Pancras station.

*Sir Thomas Beecham (1879–1961), British conductor, on Edward Elgar (1857–1934), British composer*

His wantonness is not vicious. It is that of a great baby, rather tirelessly addicted to dressing himself up as Handel or Beethoven and making a prolonged and intolerable noise.

*George Bernard Shaw (1856–1950), on Johannes Brahms (1833–97)*

What a giftless bastard!

*Pyotr Tchaikovsky (1840–93), on Johannes Brahms*

Art is long and life is short; here is evidently the explanation of a Brahms symphony.

*Edward Lorne, on Johannes Brahms*

Anton Bruckner wrote the same symphony nine times (ten actually), trying to get it right. He failed.

*Edward Abbey, American writer, on Anton Bruckner (1824–96), composer*

If he'd been making shell cases during the war it might have been better for music.

*Camille Saint-Saëns (1835–1921), on Maurice Ravel (1875–1937)*

If Beethoven's *Seventh Symphony* is not by some means abridged, it will soon fall into disuse.

*Philip Hale, Boston music critic, in 1837, on Ludwig van Beethoven (1770–1827)*

The singers and crew are not only useless in themselves but spread about at large their contagious effeminacy.

*William Cobbett (1763–1835), British journalist, agricultural reformer, soldier, and radical politician, on Italian singers in London*

# 2
# ON ART

---

What is art? Prostitution.

*Charles Baudelaire (1821–67), French poet*

Who is this chap? He drinks, he's dirty, and I know there are women in the background.

*Lord Montgomery (1887–1976), British field marshal, on Augustus John (1878–1961), British artist*

*Le Dejeuner sur l'herbe*—this is a young man's practical joke, a shameful sore not worth exhibiting in this way.

*Louis Étienne, French critic, on the painting by Edouard Manet (1832–83)*

To the service of the most wildly eccentric thoughts, he brings the acerbity of a bigot . . . his mental temperament is that of the first Spanish Grand Inquisitor. He is a Torquemada of aesthetics . . . he would burn alive the critic who disagrees with him.

*Max Nordau (1849–1923), German physician and author, on John Ruskin (1819–1900), British critic*

I have seen and heard much of Cockney impudence before now; but never expected to hear a coxcomb ask two hundred guineas for flinging a pot of paint in the public's face.

*John Ruskin (1819–1900), British critic, on James McNeill Whistler (1834–1903), American painter*

. . . [A] life passed among pictures makes not a painter—else the policeman in the National Gallery might assert himself. As well allege that he who lives in a library must needs die a poet. Let not Mr. Ruskin flatter himself that more education makes the difference between himself and the policeman when both stand gazing in the Gallery.

*James McNeill Whistler, on John Ruskin*

If people dug up remains of this civilization a thousand years hence and found Epstein's statues and that man [Havelock] Ellis, they would think we were just savages.

*Doris Lessing (b. 1919), writer, on Jacob Epstein (1880–1959), British sculptor*

He bores me. He ought to have stuck to his flying machines.

*Auguste Renoir (1841–1919), on Leonardo da Vinci (1452–1519)*

There is one thing on earth more terrible than English music, and that is English painting.

*Heinrich Heine (1797–1856), German poet and essayist*

He will never be anything but a dauber.

*Titian (c. 1490–1576), on Tintoretto (1518–94)*

Epstein is a great sculptor. I wish he would wash, but I believe Michaelangelo *never* did, so I suppose it is part of the tradition.

*Ezra Pound (1885–1972), American poet*

I mock thee not, though I by thee am mocked; Thou call'st me madman, but I call thee blockhead.

*William Blake (1757–1827), English artist and poet, on John Flaxman (1755–1826), English sculptor*

Rembrandt is not to be compared in the painting of character with our extraordinarily gifted English artist Mr. Rippingille.

*John Hunt, nineteenth-century art critic, on Rembrandt (1606–69)*

The properties of his figures are sometimes such as might be corrected by a common sign painter.

*William Hogarth (1697–1764), British painter, satirist, and engraver, on Antonio Correggio (1494–1534), Italian painter*

A monstrous orchid.

*Oscar Wilde (1854–1900), on Aubrey Beardsley (1872–98)*

He is nothing but a peeping Tom, behind the coulisses and among the dressing rooms of ballet dancers, noting only travesties on fallen womanhood, most disgusting and offensive.

> The Churchman, *on Edgar Degas (1834–1917), French painter*

Shockingly mad, madder than ever, quite mad.

> *Horace Walpole (1717–97), British letter writer and memoirist, on Henry Fuseli (1741–1825), Swiss-born British artist*

Just explain to Monsieur Renoir that the torso of a woman is not a mass of decomposing flesh, its green and violet spots indicating the state of complete putrefaction of a corpse.

> *Albert Wolff, critic, on Auguste Renoir (1841–1919)*

Mr. Lewis's pictures appeared to have been painted by a mailed fist in a cotton glove.

> *Dame Edith Sitwell (1887–1964), on Wyndham Lewis (1884–1957)*

This is not amusing, it is dismaying and disheartening. The other day, someone attributed to me the statement that "the human race was nearing insanity." I never said that but if anyone is trying to convince me that this is "modern art," and that it is representative of our time, I would be obliged to think that statement is true.

> *Kenyon Cox, American critic, in* Harper's Weekly *(1913), on Henri Matisse's painting* The Red Studio

It makes me look as if I were straining a stool.

> *Winston Churchill (1874–1965), on a portrait of him by Graham Sutherland (1903–80)*

His pictures seem to resemble not pictures but a sample book of patterns of linoleum.

> *Cyril Asquith, British critic, on Paul Klee (1879–1940), Swiss artist*

Daubaway Weirdsley.

> Punch *(February 1895), on Aubrey Beardsley (1872–98), British artist and author*

As for Monsieur Cézanne, his name will be forever linked with the most memorable artistic joke of the last fifteen years.

*Camille Mauclair, critic, on Paul Cézanne (1839–1906), French painter*

A decorator tainted with insanity.

*Kenyon Cox, American critic, in* Harper's Weekly *in 1913, on Paul Gauguin (1848–1903), French painter*

If this is art it must be ostracized as the poets were banished from Plato's republic.

*Robert Ross, British critic, in the* Morning Post *in 1910, on Vincent van Gogh (1853–90)*

Of course we all know that Morris was a wonderful all-round man, but the act of walking round him has always tired me.

*Max Beerbohm (1872–1956), on William Morris (1834–96), British poet, artist, and socialist*

Rossetti is not a painter. Rossetti is a ladies' maid.

*James McNeill Whistler, on Dante Gabriel Rossetti (1828–82), British poet and painter*

Mr. Whistler has always spelt *art* with a capital *I*.

> *Oscar Wilde (1854–1900), on James McNeill Whistler*

My dear Whistler, you leave your pictures in such a sketchy, unfinished state. Why don't you ever finish them?

> *Frederic Leighton (1830–96), British painter, on James McNeill Whistler (1834–1903), American painter*

My dear Leighton, why do you ever begin yours?

> *James McNeill Whistler, on Frederic Leighton*

I have been to it and I am pleased to find it more odious than I ever dared hope.

> *Samuel Butler (1835–1902), on a Dante Gabriel Rossetti exhibition*

It resembles a tortoiseshell cat having a fit in a plate of tomatoes.

> *Mark Twain (1835–1910), on J. M. W. Turner's* The Slave Ship

# 3
# ON ROYALTY AND ARISTOCRACY

---

George the First was always reckoned
Vile, but viler George the Second;
And what mortal ever heard
Any good from George the Third?
When from Earth the Fourth descended
(God be praised!) the Georges ended.

*Walter Savage Landor (1775–1864), English author, on the four Georges of England*

He has the heart of a cucumber fried in snow.

*Ninon de Lenclos, French courtesan, on the Marquis de Sévigné, French aristocrat*

. . . a pig, an ass, a dunghill, the spawn of an adder, a basilisk, a lying buffoon, a mad fool with a frothy mouth.

*Martin Luther (1483–1546), on Henry VIII (1491–1547)*

George the Third,
Ought never to have occurred.
One can only wonder
At so grotesque a blunder.

*Edmund Clerihew Bentley (1875–1956), on George III (1738–1820)*

The church's wet nurse, Goody Anne.

*Horace Walpole (1717–97), British letter writer and memoirist, on Queen Anne (1665–1714)*

Here lies our mutton-loving king,
Whose word no man relies on;
Who never said a foolish thing,
And never did a wise one.

*John Wilmot, Earl of Rochester, on King Charles II (1630–85)*

Queen Victoria was like a great paperweight that for half a century sat upon men's minds, and when she was removed their ideas began to blow all over the place haphazardly.

*H. G. Wells (1866–1946), on Queen Victoria (1819–1901)*

A corpulent voluptuary.

*Rudyard Kipling (1865–1936), on Edward VII (1841–1910)*

Henry VIII perhaps approached as nearly to the ideal standard of perfect wickedness as the infirmities of human nature will allow.

*Sir James Mackintosh (1765–1832), British historian, on Henry VIII (1491–1547)*

A more profligate parson I never met.

*George IV (1762–1830), on Sydney Smith (1771–1845), British clergyman, writer, and wit*

I am unwell. Bring me a glass of brandy.

*George, Prince of Wales (1762–1830), in 1795, on having kissed for the first time his bride-to-be, Princess Caroline of Brunswick (1768–1821)*

No danger. For no man in England would take away my life to make you king.

> *Charles II (1630–85), to his brother the Duke of York (1633–1701), upon being warned by him of the danger of walking about unprotected*

Now at least I know where he is.

> *Queen Alexandra (1844–1925), to Lord Esher shortly after her husband, Edward VII (1841–1910), had died*

My dear firstborn is the greatest ass, and the greatest liar and the greatest canaille and the greatest beast in the whole world and I most heartily wish he were out of it.

> *Queen Caroline (1683–1737), on her son Frederick, Prince of Wales (1707–51)*

Yes. I do think the bloom of her ugliness is going off.

> *Colonel Disbrowe, chamberlain to Queen Charlotte, wife of George III, on the slight improvement in her looks as she grew older*

She was happy as the dey was long.

*Chief Justice Lord Norbury, on Queen Caroline's affair with the Muslim Dey of Algiers in 1820*

He would fain be a Despot, even at the cost of another's Underling . . . I look on him as one of the moral Monsters of History.

*Samuel Taylor Coleridge (1772–1834), British poet, on Charles II (1630–85)*

Throughout the greater part of his life, George III was a kind of consecrated obstruction.

*Walter Bagehot (1826–77), British historian, on George III (1738–1820)*

The wisest fool in Christendom.

*Henri IV (1553–1610), first Bourbon King of France, on James I of England (1566–1625)*

A dull, stupid and profligate King, full of drink and low conversation, without dignity of appearance or manner, without sympathy of any kind with the English people and English ways and without the slightest knowledge of the English language.

*Justin McCarthy, Irish journalist and writer, on George I (1660–1727)*

Here lies Fred,
Who was alive and now is dead:
Had it been his father,
I had much rather;
Had it been his brother,
Better than another;
had it been his sister,
No one would have missed her;
Had it been the whole generation,
Better for the nation:
But since 'tis only Fred,
Who was alive and is dead–
There's no more to be said

*Horace Walpole (1717–97), English writer, on Frederick, Prince of Wales (1707–51)*

Cursed Jezebel of England.

*John Knox (1505–72), on Mary I (1516–58)*

Very sorry can't come. Lie follows by post.

*Telegram from Charles Beresford to the Prince of Wales (1894–1972), later Edward VIII, following a dinner invitation at short notice*

Alvanley—who's your fat friend?

*George Beau Brummel (1778–1840), British dandy, of George IV (1762–1830)*

Born into the ranks of the working class, the new King's most likely fate would have been that of a street-corner loafer.

*James Keir Hardie (1856–1915), British Labour Party politician, on George V (1865–1936)*

The plain truth is, that he was a most intolerable ruffian, a disgrace to human nature, and a blot of blood and grease upon the History of England.

*Charles Dickens (1812–70), on Henry VIII (1491–1547)*

You have sent me a Flanders mare.

*Henry VIII, seeing Anne of Cleves (1515–57) for the first time*

Queen Anne was one of the smallest people ever set in a great place.

*Walter Bagehot (1826–77), British historian, on Queen Anne (1665–1714)*

I cannot find it in me to fear a man who took ten years a-learning of his alphabet.

*Elizabeth I (1533–1603), on Philip II of Spain (1527–98)*

Nowadays a parlor maid as ignorant as Queen Victoria was when she came to the throne would be classed as mentally defective.

*George Bernard Shaw (1856–1950), on Queen Victoria (1819–1901)*

What is there in the delivering over of a purgid blockhead and an unprincipled prostitute into the hands of the hangman that it should arrest for a moment attention?

*Robert Burns (1759–96), on the execution of Louis XVI (1754–93) and Marie Antoinette (1755–93) of France*

King William blew his nose twice and wiped the royal perspiration from a face which is probably the largest uncivilized spot in England.

*Oliver Wendell Holmes (1809–94), American writer, on William IV (1765–1837)*

A noble, nasty course he ran,
Superbly filthy and fastidious;
He was the world's "first gentleman,"
and made the appellation hideous.

*Winthrop Mackworth Praed, on George IV (1762–1830)*

Most gracious Queen, we thee implore
To go away and sin no more,
But if that effort be too great,
to go away at any rate.

*Anonymous epigram, on Caroline of Brunswick (1768–1821), wife of George IV*

A more contemptible, cowardly, selfish unfeeling dog does not exist than this king . . . with vices and weaknesses of the lowest and most contemptible order.

*Charles Greville, English diarist, on George IV (1762–1830)*

His intellect is of no more use than a pistol packed in the bottom of a trunk in the robber-infested Apennines.

*Prince Albert (1819–61), Consort of Queen Victoria, on Edward, Prince of Wales (1841–1910)*

Who is this Pope I hear so much about? I cannot discover what is his merit. Why will my subjects not write in prose?

*George II (1683–1760), on Alexander Pope (1688–1744), British poet*

Strip your Louis Quatorze of his king gear, and there is left nothing but a poor forked radish with a head fantastically carved.

*Thomas Carlyle, Scottish historian and essayist, on Louis XIV (1638–1715)*

In private life he would have been called an honest blockhead.

*Lady Mary Wortley Montagu (1689–1762), on George I (1660–1727)*

The most notorious whore in all the world.

*Peter Wentworth, English Member of Parliament, on Mary, Queen of Scots (1542–87)*

Henry IV's feet and armpits enjoyed an international reputation.

*Aldous Huxley (1894–1963), British writer, on King Henry IV (1366–1413)*

For seventeen years he did nothing at all but kill animals and stick in stamps.

*Harold Nicolson, English diplomat and writer, while writing his biography on George V (1865–1936)*

As just and merciful as Nero and as good a Christian as Mohammed.

*John Wesley (1703–91), on Elizabeth I (1533–1603)*

Damn the North! and damn the South! and damn Wellington! The question is, how am I going to get rid of this damned Princess of Wales?

*The Prince of Wales (1762–1830), later George IV, on a political marriage for him despite his private marriage to Mrs. Fitzherbert*

# 4
# ON PROVERBS AND CURSES

---

Trust a Brahman before a snake, and a snake before a harlot, and a harlot before an Afghan.

*Traditional Hindu saying*

An Englishman will burn his bed to catch a flea.

*Traditional Turkish proverb*

Cursed be your mother's anus. Cursed be your father's testicles.

*Traditional Yoruba dueling curse*

I shit on the balls of your dead ones.

*Traditional Spanish Gypsy curse*

A waste of skin.

*Traditional Lancashire, England, expression*

Shake a bridle over a Yorkshireman's grave and he will rise and steal a horse.

*Traditional Lancashire, England, saying*

He lied like an eyewitness.

*Russian proverb*

After shaking hands with a Greek, count your fingers.

*Traditional Albanian saying*

There are only two types of Chinese—those who give bribes and those who take them.

*Russian proverb*

England: a good land and a bad people.

*Traditional French saying*

As sluttish and slatternly as an Irishwoman bred in France.

*Traditional Irish saying*

Half an Italian is one too many in a house.

*Traditional French and German insult*

Italy is a paradise inhabited by devils.

*Traditional German saying*

An ass in Germany is a professor in Rome.

*Traditional German saying*

Make one sign of the cross before an Andalusian and three on sighting a Genoese.

*Traditional Spanish saying*

A Lithuanian is not worth a cheap slipper.

*Traditional German saying*

Did hogs feed here or did Lithuanians have a feast here?

*Traditional Polish saying*

The Lithuanian is stupid like a pig but cunning like a serpent.

*Traditional Polish saying*

The devil seduced Eve in Italian. Eve misled Adam in Bohemian. The Lord scolded them both in German. Then the angel drove them from paradise in Hungarian.

*Traditional Polish saying*

A single Russian hair outweighs half a Pole.

*Traditional Russian saying*

The Pole is there to oppress and the peasant to endure.

*Traditional Ukrainian saying*

The Pole is a thief; the Prussian a traitor; the Bohemian a heretic; and the Swabian a chatterbox.

*Traditional Ukrainian saying*

The Russian knows the way, yet he asks for directions.

*Traditional German saying*

Be friendly with the Russian, but take care that you have a rock ready on your chest.

*Traditional Ukrainian saying*

May you wander over the face of the earth forever, never sleep twice in the same bed, never drink water twice from the same well, and never cross the same river twice in a year.

*Traditional Gypsy curse*

The Spaniard is a bad servant but a worse master.

*Traditional English saying*

The only good that comes from the east is the sun.

*Traditional Portuguese saying*

He who would eat in Spain must bring his kitchen along.

*Traditional German saying*

Die, may he: Tiger, catch him; Snake, bite him; Steep hill, fall down on him; River, flow over him; Wild boar, bite him.

*Traditional curse of the Todas of southern India*

God made serpents and rabbits and Armenians.

*Turkish saying*

May your left ear wither and fall into your right pocket.

*Traditional Arab curse*

May you melt off the earth like snow off the ditch.

*Traditional Irish curse*

May you dig up your father by moonlight and make soup of his bones.

*Traditional Fiji Islands curse*

May the curse of Mary Malone and her nine blind illegitimate children chase you so far over the hills of Damnation that the Lord himself can't find you with a telescope.

*Traditional Irish curse*

May you be cursed with chronic anxiety about the weather.

*John Burroughs (1837–1921)*

# 5
# ON PEOPLE AND PLACES

---

The indigested vomit of the sea
Fell to the Dutch by just propriety.

*Andrew Marvell (1621–78), English poet, in* The Character of Holland *(c. 1664)*

What a pity it is that we have no amusements in England but vice and religion.

*Sydney Smith (1771–1845), British clergyman, writer, and wit*

America is one long expectoration.

*Oscar Wilde (1854–1900)*

The way to endure Summer in England is to have it framed and glazed in a comfortable room.

*Horace Walpole (1717–97)*

There are in England sixty different religions and only one sauce.

*Carraciolo (d. 1641)*

I have been trying all my life to like Scotchmen and am obligated to desist from the experiment in despair.

*Charles Lamb (1775–1834)*

Much may be made of a Scotchman, if he be caught young.

*Samuel Johnson (1709–1784)*

Their demeanor is invariably morose, sullen, clownish, and repulsive. I should think there is not, on the face of the earth, a people so entirely destitute of humor, vivacity, or the capacity for enjoyment.

*Charles Dickens (1812–70), on Americans*

I never saw an American man walk or stand well; they are nearly all hollow chested and round shouldered.

*Frances Trollope (1780–1863), British writer*

Of course, America had often been discovered before Columbus, but it had always been hushed up.

*Oscar Wilde (1854–1900)*

If I owned Texas and Hell, I would rent out Texas and live in Hell.

*Philip H. Sheridan (1831–88), American general*

This gloomy region, where the year is divided into one day and one night, lies entirely outside the stream of history.

*W. W. Reade, in 1892, on Canada*

The purity of the air of Newfoundland is without doubt due to the fact that the people of the outports never open their windows.

*J. G. Millais (1865–1931), English painter and illustrator, in 1907, on Newfoundland, Canada*

A rascally heap of sand, rock, swamp, called Prince Edward Island, in the horrible gulf of St. Lawrence; that lump of worthlessness . . . bears nothing but potatoes.

*William Cobbett (1763–1835)*

So this is Winnipeg. I can tell it's not Paris.

*Bob Edwards (1864–1922), Scottish-born Canadian pioneer, on Winnipeg, Canada*

Niagara Falls is simply a vast, unnecessary amount of water going the wrong way and then falling over unnecessary rocks.

*Oscar Wilde (1854–1900)*

I suppose there is less alms-giving in America than in any other Christian country on the face of the globe. It is not in the temper of the people either to give or to receive.

*Frances Trollope (1780–1863)*

The American has no language. He has dialect, slang, provincialism, accent, and so forth.

*Rudyard Kipling (1865–1936)*

In Russia a man is called reactionary if he objects to having his property stolen and his wife and children murdered.

*Winston Churchill (1874–1965)*

You know that these two nations are at war for a few acres of snow, and that they are spending . . . more than all Canada is worth.

*Voltaire (1694–1778)*

The Americans, like the English, probably make love worse than any other race.

*Walt Whitman (1819–92)*

Kick all America in the guts: they need it. . . .Spit on every neurotic. . . . All that arty and literary crew, I know them, they are smoking, steaming shits.

*D. H. Lawrence (1885–1930), in a letter to Mabel Dodge Luhan, on the United States*

England, the heart of a rabbit in the body of a lion. The jaws of a serpent, in an abode of popinjays.

*Eugene Deschamps (fourteenth century), on England*

The perfidious, haughty, savage, disdainful, stupid, slothful, inhospitable, inhuman English.

*Julius Caesar Scaliger (1540–1609), on England*

You must look out in England that you are not cheated by the charioteers.

*Marcus Tullius Cicero (106–43 B.C.)*

It is related of an Englishman that he hanged himself to avoid the daily task of dressing and undressing.

*Johann Wolfgang von Goethe (1749–1832), German writer, on the English*

What I got by going to Canada was a cold.

*Henry David Thoreau (1817–62)*

Our nation is divided into two species: the one of idle monkeys who mock at everything; and the other of tigers who tear.

*Voltaire (1694–1778), on France*

It is by the goodness of God that in our country we have those three unspeakably precious things: freedom of speech, freedom of conscience, and the prudence never to practice either of them.

*Mark Twain (1835–1910)*

America . . . where laws and customs alike are based on the dreams of spinsters.

*Bertrand Russell (1872–1970), English mathematician and philosopher*

In unimportant trifles, he deals in the most puerile and endless distinctions, while in matters of utility not to say matters of science, it [the Javanese language] is utterly defective. . . . It wantons in exuberance, when species, varieties, and individuals are described—while no skill is displayed in combining and generalizing.

*John Crawford, orientalist and colonial administrator, in 1820, on the Javanese language*

The Javans' income is frittered away by being wasted on the vile herd of miscreants and vagabonds belonging to the Hindu village under the various and incongruous appellations of astronomers, doctors, poets, musicians, barbers, and dancing girls.

*John Crawford, in 1820, comparing the Javanese peasant to the Hindu peasant*

Lazy and listless . . . they rise about half past seven or eight o'clock in the morning. They spend the forenoon in toying and playing with their female slaves while a few moments afterward they will have the poor creatures whipped most unmercifully for the merest trifle. They loll in a loose and airy dress upon the sofa.

*John Crawford, in 1820, on the offspring of oriental female slaves and Europeans in the Dutch East Indies*

We know no spectacle so ridiculous as the British public in one of its periodical fits of morality.

*Thomas Babington Macaulay (1800–59), British historian*

England and America are two countries divided by a common language.

*Attributed to George Bernard Shaw (1856–1950)*

One thing I will say for the Germans, they are always perfectly willing to give somebody else's land to somebody else.

*Will Rogers (1879–1935), American humorist*

"English Fair Play" is a fine expression. It justifies the bashing of the puny draper's assistant by the big hairy blacksmith, and this to the perfect satisfaction of both parties, if they are worthy of the name of Englishman.

*Joseph Furphy, Australian novelist, in 1903*

The English are the people of consummate cant.

*Friedrich Wilhelm Nietzsche (1844–1900), German philosopher*

The English never smash in a face. They merely refrain from asking it to dinner.

*Margaret Hasley, American writer*

# 6
# ON HISTORIANS

---

I spent a horrid, horrid night. I dreamt I was chained to a rock and being talked to death by Harriet Martineau and Macaulay.

> *Sydney Smith (1771–1845), on Harriet Martineau (1802–76), British feminist, philanthropist, and writer, and Thomas Babington Macaulay (1800–59), British historian*

The great apostle of the Philistines.

> *Matthew Arnold (1822–88), on Thomas Babington Macaulay*

You know, when I am gone, you will be sorry you never heard me speak.

*Sydney Smith, to the notoriously garrulous Thomas Babington Macaulay*

He not only overfilled with learning but stood in the slop.

*Thomas Carlyle (1795–1881), on Thomas Babington Macaulay*

The same old sausage, fizzing and sputtering in its own grease.

*Henry James (1843–1916), on Thomas Carlyle*

Another thick square book! Always scribble, scribble, scribble! Eh! Mr. Gibbon!

*William, Duke of Gloucester, to Edward Gibbon (1737–94)*

Gibbon is an ugly, affected, disgusting fellow and poisons our literary club for me. I class him among infidel wasps and venomous insects.

*James Boswell, on Edward Gibbon*

Gibbon's style is detestable; but it is not the worst thing about him.

*Samuel Taylor Coleridge (1772–1834), British poet, on Edward Gibbon*

# 7
# ON POLITICIANS

---

They told me how Mr. Gladstone read Homer for fun, which I thought served him right.

*Winston Churchill (1874–1965), on William Ewart Gladstone (1809–98)*

It was said Mr. Gladstone could convince most people of most things, and himself of anything.

*Dean William R. Inge, on William Ewart Gladstone*

Brilliant to the top of his army boots.

*David Lloyd George (1863–1945), on Douglas Haig (1861–1928), British field marshal*

Oh, if I could piss the way he speaks!

*Georges Clemenceau (1841–1929), on David Lloyd George*

If he were a horse, nobody would buy him; with that eye, no one could answer for his temper.

*Walter Bagehot (1826–77), British historian, on Lord Henry Peter Brougham (1778–1868), British statesman and author*

One could drive a schooner through any part of his argument and never scrape against a fact.

*David Houston, American politician, on William Jennings Bryan (1860–1925), American lawyer and politician*

A lamentably successful cross between a fox and a hog.

*James G. Blaine, American politician, on Benjamin Franklin Butler (1818–93), American soldier*

A Winston Churchill who had never been to Harrow.

*H. G. Wells (1866–1946), on Huey P. Long (1893–1935), American politician*

Dr. Dread-Devil . . . said that there were no trees in Scotland. I wonder how they managed to take him around without letting him see trees. I suppose that that lick-spittle Boswell, or Mrs. Piozzi, tied a bandage over his eyes when he went over the country which I have been over. I shall sweep away at this bundle of lies.

*William Cobbett (1763–1835), on Samuel Johnson (1709–84)*

God damn your god damned old hellfired god damned soul to hell god damn you and god damn your god damned family's god damned hellfired god damned soul to hell and good damnation god damn them and god damn your god damned friends to hell.

*Peter Muggins, American citizen, in a letter to President Abraham Lincoln (1809–65)*

Filthy Story-Teller, Despot, Liar, Thief, Braggart, Buffoon, Usurper, Monster, Ignoramus Abe, Old Scoundrel, Perjurer, Robber, Swindler, Tyrant, Field-Butcher, Land-Pirate.

Harper's Weekly, *on Abraham Lincoln*

You and I were long friends; you are now my enemy and I am Yours,
Benjamin Franklin

*Benjamin Franklin (1706–1790), to William Strahan*

With death doomed to grapple
Beneath this cold slab, he
Who lied in the Chapel
Now lies in the Abbey.

*Lord Byron (1788–1824), on William Pitt (1759–1806)*

That dark designing sordid ambitious vain proud arrogant and vindictive knave.

*General Charles Lee (1731–83), on George Washington (1732–99)*

. . . [A]nd to you, sir, treacherous in private friendship . . . and a hypocrite in public life, the world will be puzzled to decide whether you are an apostate or an impostor, whether you have abandoned good principles or whether you ever had any.

*Thomas Paine (1737–1809), in a letter to George Washington*

He was essentially a prig, and among prigs there is a freemasonry which never fails. All the prigs spoke of him as the coming man.

*Benjamin Disraeli (1840–81), on William Ewart Gladstone (1809–98)*

He has committed every crime that does not require courage.

*Benjamin Disraeli, on Daniel O'Connell (1775–1847), Irish lawyer, politician, and agitator*

Douglas can never be president, Sir. No, Sir; Douglas never can be president, Sir. His legs are too short, Sir. His coat, like a cow's tail, hangs too near the ground, Sir.

*Thomas Hart Benton (1782–1858), American artist, on Stephen A. Douglas, presidential candidate*

Wallowing in corruption like a rhinoceros in an African pool.

*E. L. Godkin (1831–1902), American journalist and author, on James G. Blaine, American politician*

He was oppressed by metaphor, dislocated by parentheses, and debilitated by amplification.

*Samuel Parr (1747–1825), English scholar, on a speech by Edmund Burke (1729–97)*

. . . [H]e insults the House of Lords and plagues the most eminent of his colleagues with the crabbed malice of a maundering witch.

*Benjamin Disraeli (1804–81), on the Earl of Aberdeen (1784–1860)*

They inculcate the morals of a whore and the manners of a dancing master.

*Samuel Johnson (1709–84), on Lord Chesterfield's letters of advice to his son*

He is like a carving knife whetted on a brickbat.

*John Randolph (1773–1833), American politician, on Ben Harden, American politician*

His face is ashen, gaunt his whole body,
His breath is green with gall;
His tongue drips poison.

*Ovid (43 B.C.–A.D. 17), applied by John Quincy Adams (1767–1848) to John Randolph*

Every drop of blood in that man's veins has eyes that look downward.

*Ralph Waldo Emerson (1803–82), American philosopher and poet, on Daniel Webster (1782–1852), American politician*

We did not conceive it possible that even Mr. Lincoln would produce a paper so slipshod, so loose-joined, so puerile, not alone in literary construction, but in its ideas, its sentiments, its grasp. He has outdone himself.

Chicago Times *on President Abraham Lincoln's November 19, 1863, Gettysburg Address*

A crafty and lecherous old hypocrite whose very statue seems to gloat on the wenches as they walk the States House yard.

*William Cobbett (1763–1835), on Benjamin Franklin (1706–90)*

He has all the characteristics of a dog except loyalty.

*Sam Houston, American politician, on Thomas Jefferson Green (1801–63), American politician*

He has a bungalow mind.

*Woodrow Wilson (1856–1924), twenty-eighth American president, on Warren Harding (1865–1923), twenty-ninth American president*

The General is suffering from mental saddle sores.

*Harold L. Ickes, American Secretary of the Interior, on Hugh S. Johnson (1882–1942), American soldier*

The style of all pestilential filth that hath infested the state and government of this commonwealth.

*Sir Harbottle Grimston, British Member of Parliament, on William Laud (1573–1645), English clergyman and Archbishop of Canterbury*

Gladstone appears to me one of the contemptibilist men I ever looked on. A poor Ritualist; almost spectral kind of phantasm of a man.

*Thomas Carlyle (1795–1881), Scottish historian and essayist, on William Ewart Gladstone (1809–98)*

What is that fat man in such a passion about?

*Lord Eversley as a child in the gallery of the House of Commons, in G. W. E. Russell's* Collections and Recollections *(1898), on Charles James Fox (1749–1806), British statesman*

You show the bourgeoisie your behind. We, on the contrary, look them in the face.

*Georgi Plekhanov, Russian Social Democrat, on Vladimir Ilyich Lenin (1870–1942), Soviet leader*

Like rotten mackerel by moonlight, he shines and stinks.

*John Randolph, American politician, on Edward Livingstone (1764–1836), American politician*

He is a self-made man and worships his creator.

*Attributed to John Bright, on Benjamin Disraeli (1804–81)*

If a traveler were informed that such a man was the leader of the House of Commons, he might begin to comprehend how the Egyptians worshiped an insect.

*Benjamin Disraeli (1804–81), British prime minister and author, on Lord John Russell (1792–1878), British prime minister*

His impact on history would be no more than the whiff of scent on a lady's handkerchief.

*David Lloyd George (1863–1945), on Arthur Balfour (1848–1930)*

My one ardent desire is that after the war he should be publicly castrated in front of Nurse Cavell's statue.

*Lytton Strachey (1880–1932), British writer, on David Lloyd George*

I thought him fearfully ill educated and quite tenth rate—pathetic. I felt quite maternal to him.

*Hugh Walpole (1884–1941), on meeting Adolf Hitler (1889–1945), in 1925*

His smile is like the silver fittings on a coffin.

*Benjamin Disraeli (1804–81), on Robert Peel (1788–1850)*

He only had one idea and that was wrong.

*Benjamin Disraeli, on a now-forgotten British Member of Parliament*

He is a mere cork, dancing in a current which he cannot control.

*Arthur Balfour (1848–1930), British prime minister, on Henry Campbell-Bannerman (1836–1908), British prime minister*

Not a gentleman. Dresses too well.

*Bertrand Russell (1872–1970), on Anthony Eden (1895–1977)*

He spent his whole life in plastering together the true and the false and therefrom manufacturing the plausible.

*Stanely Baldwin (1867–1947), on David Lloyd George (1863–1945)*

Sir Stafford has a brilliant mind until it is made up.

*Lady Violet Bonham-Carter (1887–1969), on Sir Stafford Cripps (1889–1952)*

I met murder on the way—
He had a mask like Castlereagh.

*Percy Bysshe Shelley (1792–1822), on Viscount Castlereagh (1769–1822), British foreign minister from 1812 to 1822*

Posterity will ne'er survey
A nobler grave than this;
Here lie the bones of Castlereagh:
Stop, traveller, and piss.

*Lord Byron (1788–1824), on Viscount Castlereagh*

Mr. Gladstone speaks to me as if I were a public meeting.

*Queen Victoria (1819–1901), on William Ewart Gladstone (1809–98)*

I thought he was a young man of promise; but it appears he was a young man of promises.

*Arthur James Balfour (1848–1930), on Winston Churchill (1874–1965)*

Like a cushion he always bore the impress of the last man who had sat on him.

*David Lloyd George, on Lord Derby (1865–1948); also attributed to Lord Haig*

This goat-footed bard, this half-human visitor to our age from the hag-ridden magic and enchanted woods of Celtic antiquity.

*John Maynard Keynes (1883–1946), on David Lloyd George (1863–1945)*

The right honorable and learned gentleman has twice crossed the floor of this House, each time leaving behind a trail of slime.

*David Lloyd George, on Sir John Simon (1873–1954)*

I think Baldwin has gone mad. He simply takes one jump in the dark; looks around and then takes another.

*Lord Birkenhead (1872–1930), on Stanley Baldwin (1867–1947)*

A tardy little marionette.

*Randolph Churchill (1849–95), on Clement Attlee (1883–1967)*

If Kitchener was not a great man, he was at least, a great poster.

*Margot Asquith (1864–1945), on Lord Kitchener (1850–1916)*

One could not even dignify him with the name of a stuffed shirt. He was simply a hole on the air.

*George Orwell (1903–50), on Stanley Baldwin (1867–1947)*

Stupid asses.

*Karl Marx (1818–83), to Friedrich Engels (1820–95), in private correspondence, on the proletariat*

That grand impostor, that loathsome hypocrite, that detestable traitor, that prodigy of nature, that opprobrium of mankind, that landscape of iniquity, that sink of sin, that compendium of baseness who now calls himself our Protector.

*Anabaptists' address to Charles II, on Oliver Cromwell (1599–1658), Lord Protector of England*

He lived a hypocrite and died a traitor.

*John Foster, English historian, on Oliver Cromwell*

. . . [A]s thin as the homeopathic soup that was made by boiling the shadow of a pigeon that had been starved to death.

*Abraham Lincoln (1809–65), on the ability of Stephen A. Douglas, American politician, to reason*

He is a silk stocking filled with dung.

*Napoléon Bonaparte (1769–1821), on Charles Maurice de Talleyrand Périgord (1754–1838), French statesman and diplomat*

A cold-blooded, calculating, unprincipled usurper, without a virtue; no statesman, knowing nothing of commerce, political economy, or civil government, and supplying ignorance by bold presumption.

*Thomas Jefferson (1743–1826), American president, on Napoléon Bonaparte*

If Gladstone fell into the Thames, that would be a misfortune, and if anybody pulled him out that, I supposed, would be a calamity.

*Benjamin Disraeli (1804–81), British prime minister, on rival prime minister William Ewart Gladstone (1809–98)*

The manners of a cad and the tongue of a bargee.

*Herbert Asquith (1852–1928), British prime minister, on Joseph Chamberlain (1836–1914), British politician*

Listening to a speech by Chamberlain is like paying a visit to Woolworth's; everything in its place and nothing above sixpence.

*Aneurin Bevan (1897–1960), on Neville Chamberlain (1869–1940), British prime minister*

What other man within the walls of Parliament, however hasty, rude and petulant, hath exhibited such manifold instances of bad manners, bad feelings, bad reasonings, bad language, and bad law?

*Walter Savage Landor (1775–1864), British poet, on Henry Peter Brougham (1778–1868), British statesman and author*

He would kill his own mother just so that he could use her skin to make a drum to beat his own praises.

*Margot Asquith (1864–1945), writer and wife of Prime Minister Herbert Henry Asquith, on Winston Churchill (1874–1965)*

A retail mind in a wholesale business.

*David Lloyd George (1863–1945), on Neville Chamberlain (1869–1940)*

Winston has devoted the best years of his life to preparing his impromptu speeches.

*F. E. Smith (1872–1930), on Winston Churchill (1874–1965)*

Dear Randolph, utterly unspoilt by failure.

*Noël Coward (1899–1973), on Randolph Churchill (1849–95)*

He occasionally stumbled over the truth, but hastily picked himself up and hurried on as if nothing had happened.

*Winston Churchill, on Stanley Baldwin (1867–1947), British statesman*

I met Curzon in Downing Street, from whom I got the sort of greeting a corpse would give to an undertaker.

*Attributed to Stanley Baldwin, on Lord Curzon (1859–1925), British statesman*

His idea of getting hold of the right tend of the stick is to snatch it from the hands of somebody who is using it effectively, and to hit him over the head with it.

*George Bernard Shaw (1856–1950), on Theodore Roosevelt (1858–1919)*

He objected to ideas only when others had them.

*A. J. P. Taylor, British historian, on Ernest Bevin (1881–1951), British politician*

Reader, suppose you were an idiot; and suppose you were a member of Congress; but I repeat myself.

*Mark Twain (1835–1910)*

You've no idea what it costs to keep the old man in poverty.

*Lord Louis Mountbatten (1900–79), on Mahatma Gandhi (1869–1948)*

As he rose like a rocket, he fell like a stick.

*Thomas Paine (1737–1809), British political philosopher, on Edmund Burke (1729–97), British author and statesman*

He slept more than any other president, whether by day or night. Nero fiddled, but Coolidge only snored.

*H. L. Mencken (1880–1956), American journalist, on Calvin Coolidge (1872–1933), American president*

How can they tell?

*Dorothy Parker (1893–1967), upon hearing that Calvin Coolidge had died*

I am sir, for the last time in my life, Your Humble Servant Horace Walpole.

*Horace Walpole (1717–97), British prime minister, ending a letter to an uncle with whom he had quarreled*

As an intellectual he bestowed upon the games of golf and bridge all the enthusiasm and perseverance that he withheld from books and ideas.

*Emmet Hughes, American writer, on Dwight Eisenhower (1890–1969), thirty-fourth American president*

He couldn't see a belt without hitting below it.

*Margot Asquith (1864–1945), on David Lloyd George (1863–1945), British prime minister*

. . . [O]nly a frantic pair of moustaches.

*T. E. Lawrence (1888–1935), on Ferdinand Foch (1851–1929), French marshal*

The Right Honorable Gentleman is indebted to his memory for his jests and to his imagination for his facts.

*Richard Brinsley Sheridan (1751–1816), Irish playwright and politician, on Henry Dundas (1742–1811), British politician*

He brings to the fierce struggle of politics the tepid enthusiasm of a lazy summer afternoon at a cricket match.

*Aneurin Bevan (1897–1960), on Clement Attlee (1883–1967), British prime minister*

Chamberlain is no better than a Mayor of Birmingham, and in a lean year at that.

*Lord Hugh Cecil, on Neville Chamberlain (1869–1940)*

He thinks himself deaf because he no longer hears himself talked of.

*Charles Maurice de Talleyrand-Périgord (1754–1838), on Vicomte de Chateaubriand (1768–1848)*

Garfield has shown that he is not possessed of the backbone of an angleworm.

*Ulysses S. Grant (1822–85), eighteenth American president, on James A. Garfield (1831–81), twentieth American president*

The people are tired of a man who has not an idea above a horse or a cigar.

*Joseph Brown, on Ulysses S. Grant*

He writes the worst English that I have ever encountered. It reminds me of a string of wet sponges; it reminds me of tattered washing on the line; it reminds me of stale bean soup, of college yells, of dogs barking idiotically through endless nights. It is so bad that a sort of grandeur creeps into it. It drags itself out of the dark abysm of pish and crawls insanely up the topmost pinnacle of posh. It is rumble and bumble. It is flap and doodle. It is balder and dash.

*H. L. Mencken (1880–1956), on Warren G. Harding (1865–1923), American president*

He's thin, boys. He's thin as piss on a hot rock.

*Senator William E. Jenner of Indiana (1908–85), on W. Averell Harriman (1891–1986), governor of New York*

He did not seem to care which way he traveled, as long as he was in the driver's seat.

*Lord Beaverbrook (1879–1964), on David Lloyd George (1863–1945)*

The moral character of Jefferson was repulsive. Continually puling about liberty, equality, and the degrading curse of slavery, he brought his own children to the hammer, and made money of his debaucheries.

*Alexander Hamilton (1757–1804), American politician, on Thomas Jefferson (1743–1826) third American president*

# 8
# ON WRITERS

---

I think of Mr. Stevenson as a consumptive youth weaving garlands of sad flowers with pale, weak hands.

> *George Moore (1852–1923), on Robert Louis Stevenson (1850–94)*

He has a gross and repulsive face but appears *bon enfant* when you talk to him. But he is the dullest Briton of them all.

> *Henry James (1843–1916), on Anthony Trollope (1815–82)*

I doubt that the infant monster has any more to give.

> *Henry James, on Rudyard Kipling (1865–1936)*

A hack writer who would not have been considered a fourth rate in Europe, who tricked out a few of the old proven "sure-fire" literary skeletons with sufficient local color to intrigue the superficial and the lazy.

*William Faulkner (1897–1962), on Mark Twain (1835–1910)*

To me Pound remains the exquisite showman minus the show.

*Ben Hecht (1894–1964), American newspaper reporter, on Ezra Pound (1885–1972)*

Literature cannot be the business of a woman's life, because of the sacredness of her duties at home.

*Robert Southey (1774–1843), on Charlotte Brontë (1816–55)*

One of the surest signs of his genius is that women dislike his books.

*George Orwell (1903–50), on Joseph Conrad (1857–1924)*

One could always baffle Conrad by saying “humor.”

*H. G. Wells (1866–1946), on Joseph Conrad*

Tell me, when you’re alone with Max, does he take off his face and reveal his mask?

*Oscar Wilde (1854–1900), on Max Beerbohm (1872–1956)*

He is the bully on the Left Bank, always ready to twist the milksop’s arm.

*Cyril Connolly (1903–74), English writer and literary critic, on Ernest Hemingway (1899–1961)*

Never have I read such tosh. As for the first two chapters, we will let them pass, but the third, the fourth the fifth the sixth—merely the scratchings of pimples on the body of the boot-boy at Claridges.

*Virginia Woolf (1882–1941), on James Joyce’s* Ulysses

We have met too late. You are too old for me to have any effect on you.

*James Joyce (1882–1941), to W. B. Yeats (1865–1939)*

Obsessed with self. Dead eyes and a red beard, long narrow face. A strange bird.

*John Galsworthy (1867–1933), on D. H. Lawrence (1885–1930)*

Books seem to me to be pestilent things, and infect all that trade in them . . . with something very perverse and brutal. Printers, binders, sellers, and others that make a trade and gain out of them, have universally so odd a turn and corruption of mind that they have a way of dealing peculiar to themselves and not conform to the good of society and that general fairness which cements mankind.

*John Locke (1632–1704), British philosopher*

Bennett—sort of a pig in clover.

*D. H. Lawrence (1885–1930), on Arnold Bennett (1867–1931), British novelist*

I have discovered that our great favourite, Miss Austen, is my countrywoman . . . with whom mamma before her marriage was acquainted. 'Mamma says that she was then the prettiest, silliest, most affected husband hunting butterfly she ever remembers.

*Mary Russell Mitford, in an April 3, 1815, letter to Sir William Elford, on Jane Austen (1775–1817)*

One of the most extraordinary successes in the history of civilization was achieved by an idler, a lecher, a drunkard, and a snob, nor was this success of that sudden explosive kind. It was the supreme expression of an entire life.

*Lytton Strachey (1880–1932), on James Boswell (1740–95), British author and biographer*

Sitting in a sewer and adding to it.

*Thomas Carlyle (1795–1881), Scottish historian and essayist, on Algernon Charles Swinburne (1837–1909), British poet*

I hate the whole race of them, there never existed a more worthless set than Byron and his friends.

*Duke of Wellington (1769–1852), on Lord Byron (1788–1824)*

He grew up from manhood into boyhood.

*R. A. Knox (1888–1957), on G. K. Chesterton (1874–1936)*

Coleridge was a muddle-headed metaphysician who by some strange streak of fortune turned out a few poems amongst the dreary flood of inanity that was his wont.

*William Morris (1834–96), on Samuel Taylor Coleridge (1772–1834)*

He has plenty of music in him, but he cannot get it out.

*Alfred, Lord Tennyson (1809–92), on Robert Browning (1812–89)*

. . . [A] flabby lemon and pink giant, who hung his mouth open as though he were an animal at the zoo inviting buns—especially when the ladies were present.

*Wyndham Lewis (1882–1957), on Ford Madox Ford (1873–1939)*

I wish her characters would talk a little less like the heroes and heroines of police reports.

*George Eliot (1819–80), on Charlotte Brontë in* Jane Eyre

All the faults of *Jane Eyre* are magnified thousand-fold and the only consolation which we have in reflecting upon it, is that it will never be generally read.

*James Lorimer, British critic, on Emily Brontë's* Wuthering Heights

Mrs. Browning's death is rather a relief to me, I must say. No more Aurora Leighs, thank God!

*Edward Fitzgerald, British poet, on Elizabeth Barrett Browning (1806–61)*

A fungus of pendulous shape.

*Alice James, on George Eliot, pseudonym of British novelist Mary Ann Evans (1819–80)*

George Eliot had the heart of Sappho; but the face, with the long proboscis, the protruding teeth of the Apocalyptic horse, betrayed animality.

*George Meredith (1828–1909), British novelist and poet, on George Eliot*

The very pimple of the age's humbug.

*Nathaniel Hawthorne (1804–64), American writer, on Edward Bulwer-Lytton (1803–73), British dandy and novelist*

I wonder that he is not thrashed; but his littleness is his protection, no man shoots a wren.

*William Broome, British poet, on Alexander Pope (1688–1744)*

A village explained. Excellent if you were a village, but if you were not, not.

*Gertrude Stein (1874–1946), on Ezra Pound (1885–1972)*

A flat flabby little person with the face of a baker, the clothes of a cobbler, the size of a barrelmaker, the manners of a stocking salesman, and the dress of an innkeeper.

*Victor de Balabin, on Honoré de Balzac (1799–1850)*

. . . [A] gap-toothed and hoary ape, who now in his dotage spits and chatters from a dirtier perch of his own finding, and fouling; coryphaeus or choragus of his Bulgarian tribe of autocoprophagaus baboons.

*Algernon Charles Swinburne (1837–1909), on Ralph Waldo Emerson (1803–82)*

If he hides in a quarry he puts reds flags all round.

*George Bernard Shaw (1856–1950), on T. E. Lawrence (1888–1935), writer and adventurer*

He's impossible. He's pathetic and preposterous. He writes like a sick man.

*Gertrude Stein (1874–1946), on D. H. Lawrence (1885–1930)*

Reading him is like wading through glue.

*Alfred, Lord Tennyson (1809–92), on Ben Jonson (1572–1637)*

So grave, sententious, dogmatical a Rogue, that there is no enduring him.

*Jonathan Swift (1667–1745), satirist and writer, on Daniel Defoe (1660–1731)*

A totally disinherited waif.

*George Santayana (1863–1952), American philosopher, on Charles Dickens (1812–70)*

He has never played any significant part in any movement more significant than that of a fly . . . on a wheel.

Saturday Review *(1857), on Charles Dickens*

Of Dickens's style it is impossible to speak in praise. It is jerky, ungrammatical, and created by himself in defiance of rules. . . . No young novelist should ever dare to imitate the style of Dickens.

*Anthony Trollope (1815–82), on Charles Dickens, in his* Autobiography *(1883)*

Mr. Eliot is at times an excellent poet and has arrived at the supreme Eminence among English critics largely through disguising himself as a corpse.

*Ezra Pound (1885–1972), on T. S. Eliot (1888–1965)*

Pale, marmoreal Eliot was there last week, like a chapped office boy on a high stool, with a cold in his head.

*Virginia Woolf (1882–1941), on T. S. Eliot*

Henry James has a mind—a sensibility—so fine that no mere idea could ever penetrate it.

*T. S. Eliot, on Henry James (1843–1916)*

Emerson's writing has a cold, cheerless glitter, like the new furniture in a warehouse, which will come of use by and by.

*Alexander Smith, American writer, in* Dreamthorp *(1864), on Ralph Waldo Emerson (1803–1882), American essayist and poet*

One of the seven humbugs of Xtiandom.

*William Morris (1835–96), British designer and writer, on Ralph Waldo Emerson*

There are two ways of disliking poetry; one way is to dislike it, the other is to read Pope.

*Oscar Wilde (1854–1900), on Alexander Pope (1688–1744)*

His manners are ninety-nine in a hundred singularly repulsive.

*Samuel Taylor Coleridge (1772–1834), on William Hazlitt (1778–1830), British essayist*

He is not a proper person to be admitted into respectable society, being the most perverse and malevolent creature that ill-luck has thrown my way.

*William Wordsworth (1770–1850), poet, on William Hazlitt*

An unattractive man with an apple-green complexion.

*Steven Runciman, British historian, on André Gide (1869–1951), French writer*

Hardy became a sort of village atheist brooding and blaspheming over the village idiot.

*G. K. Chesterton (1874–1936), British writer, on Thomas Hardy (1840–1928), British novelist and poet*

No one has written worse English than Mr. Hardy in some of his novels—cumbrous, stilted, ugly, and inexpressive—yes.

*Virginia Woolf (1882–1941), on Thomas Hardy*

All raw, uncooked, protesting.

*Virginia Woolf, on Aldous Huxley (1894–1963), British writer*

The stupid person's idea of the clever person.

*Elizabeth Bowen (1899–1973), British writer, in* The Spectator *(1936), on Aldous Huxley*

Without being intentionally obscene, he is thoroughly filthy, and has not the slightest sense of decency. In an old writer, and especially one of that age, I never saw so large a proportion of what may truly be called either trash or ordure.

*Robert Southey (1774–1843), poet laureate, in* Commonplace Book *(1812), on Robert Herrick (1592–1674), English poet*

One of the nicest old ladies I ever met.

*William Faulkner (1897–1962), on Henry James (1843–1916)*

Mr. Kipling . . . stands for everything in this cankered world which I would wish were otherwise.

*Dylan Thomas (1914–53), Welsh poet, on Rudyard Kipling (1865–1936)*

Mr. Lawrence looked like a plaster gnome on a stone toadstool in some suburban garden . . . he looked as if he had just returned from spending an uncomfortable night in a very dark cave.

*Dame Edith Sitwell (1887–1964), British author and poet, on D. H. Lawrence (1885–1930)*

Crude, immoral, vulgar, and senseless.

*Leo Tolstoy (1828–1910), on William Shakespeare (1564–1616)*

Shakespeare—what trash are his works in the gross.

*Edward Young, British poet, in 1820*

To think of him dribbling his powerful intellect through the gimlet holes of poetry.

*Thomas Carlyle (1795–1881), on Alfred, Lord Tennyson (1809–92)*

His mind is so vile a mind, so cozy, hypocritical, praise-mad, canting, envious, concupiscent.

*Samuel Taylor Coleridge (1772–1834), British poet, on Samuel Richardson (1689–1761), British novelist*

Sir, he was dull in company, dull in his closet, dull everywhere. He was dull in a new way and that made people think him great.

*Samuel Johnson (1709–84), on Thomas Gray (1716–71), British poet*

Those base, servile, self-graded wretches, Virgil and Horace.

*William Cobbett (1763–1835), on the Classical poets Virgil (70–19 B.C.) and Horace (65–8 B.C.)*

Virginia Woolf's writing is no more than glamorous knitting. I believe she must have a pattern somewhere.

*Dame Edith Sitwell (1887–1964), on Virginia Woolf (1882–1941)*

I'm sure the poor woman meant well, but I wish she'd stick to recreating the glory that was Greece and not muck about with dear old modern homos.

*Noël Coward (1899–1973), on Mary Renault (1905–1983), British novelist best known for her historical fiction about ancient Greece*

An animated adenoid.

*Norman Douglas (1868–1952), English novelist, on Ford Madox Ford (1873–1939)*

A lewd vegetarian.

*Charles Kingsley (1819–75), on Percy Bysshe Shelley (1792–1822)*

An idiot child screaming in a hospital.

*H. G. Wells (1866–1946), on George Bernard Shaw (1856–1950)*

Filth. Nothing but obscenities.

*Joseph Conrad (1857–1924), on D. H. Lawrence (1855–1930)*

Owen's tiny corpus is perhaps the most overrated poetry in the twentieth century.

*Craig Raine, British poet, on Wilfred Owen (1893–1918), British poet*

We invite people like that to tea, but we don't marry them.

*Lady Chetwode, on her future son-in-law, John Betjeman (1906–84), British poet*

Living almost always among intellectuals, she preserved to the age of fifty-six that contempt for ideas which is normal among boys and girls of fifteen.

*Odell Sheperd, American writer, on Louisa May Alcott (1832–88), American novelist*

T. S. Eliot and I like to play, but I like to play euchre, while he likes to play Eucharist.

*Robert Frost (1874–1963), on T. S. Eliot (1888–1965)*

His imagination resembles the wings of an ostrich.

*Thomas Babington Macaulay (1800–59), British historian, on John Dryden (1631–1700), English poet*

He has the most remarkable and seductive genius—and I should say about the smallest in the world.

*Lytton Strachey (1880–1932), British writer, on Max Beerbohm (1872–1956), British author and cartoonist*

What is Conrad but the wreck of Stevenson floating about in the slipsop of Henry James?

*George Moore (1852–1933), on Joseph Conrad (1857–1924)*

His verse . . . is the beads without the string.

*Gerard Manley Hopkins (1844–89), on Robert Browning (1812–89)*

. . . [A] sort of gutless Kipling.

*George Orwell (1903–50), on W. H. Auden (1907–73)*

The cynic parasite.

*Benjamin Disraeli (1804–81), on William Makepeace Thackeray (1811–63), British novelist and critic*

. . . [A] tub of old guts.

*Ezra Pound (1885–1972), on Gertrude Stein (1874–1946)*

A hyena that wrote poetry on tombs.

*Friedrich Wilhelm Nietzsche (1844–1900), on Dante (1265–1321)*

A monster, gibbering, shrieking, and gnashing imprecations against mankind.

*William Makepeace Thackeray (1811–63), on Jonathan Swift (1667–1745)*

What an old covered wagon she is.

*F. Scott Fitzgerald (1896–1940), on Gertrude Stein (1874–1946)*

A tadpole of the lakes.

*Lord Byron (1788–1824), on John Keats (1795–1821)*

With the single exception of Homer, there is no eminent writer, not even Sir Walter Scott, whom I can despise so entirely as I despise Shakespeare when I measure my mind against his . . . it would positively be a relief to me to dig him up and throw stones at him.

*George Bernard Shaw (1856–1950), on William Shakespeare (1564–1616)*

He is all blood, dirt, and sucked sugar stick.

*W. B. Yeats (1865–1939), on Wilfred Owen (1893–1918)*

She looked like Lady Chatterley above the waist and the gamekeeper below.

*Cyril Connolly (1903–74), on Vita Sackville-West (1892–1962)*

He is all ice and woodenfaced acrobatics.

*Wyndham Lewis (1882–1957), on W. H. Auden (1907–73)*

I want words sufficient to express thy viperous Treason . . . there never lived a viler viper on the face of the earth than thou.

*Sir Edward Coke (1552–1634), to Sir Walter Raleigh (1552–1618), Elizabethan writer, courtier, and explorer*

A dirty man with opium-glazed eyes and rat-taily hair.

*Lady Frederick Cavendish, British aristocrat, on Alfred, Lord Tennyson (1809–92)*

A man carved from a turnip looking out from astonished eyes.

*W. B. Yeats (1865–1939), on George Moore (1852–1933), Anglo-Irish novelist*

This enormous dunghill.

*Voltaire (1694–1778), on William Shakespeare (1564–1616)*

The godless arch scoundrel Voltaire is dead—dead like a dog, like a beast.

*Wolfgang Amadeus Mozart (1756–91)*

A great cow full of ink.

*Gustave Flaubert (1821–80), on George Sand (1804–76)*

Thackeray settled like a meat-fly on whatever one had got for dinner; and made one sick of it.

*John Ruskin (1819–1900), on William Makepeace Thackeray (1811–63)*

A reptile marking his path wherever he goes and breathing a mildew at everything fresh and fragrant; a midnight ghoul preying on rottenness and repulsive filth. A creature hated by his nearest intimates and bearing his consciousness thereof upon his distorted features and upon his despicable soul.

*Walt Whitman (1819–91), on James Gordon Bennett,* New York Herald *editor*

The enemy of all mankind, you are, full of the lust of enmity. It is not the hatred of falsehood which inspires you. It is the hatred of people, of flesh and blood. It is a perverted blood lust, why don't you own it?

*D. H. Lawrence (1885–1930), on Bertrand Russell (1872–1970)*

He is the old maid among novelists.

*Dame Rebecca West (1892–1983), on H. G. Wells (1866–1946)*

Is Wordsworth a bell with a wooden tongue?

*Ralph Waldo Emerson (1803–82), on William Wordsworth (1770–1850)*

Jane Austen's books, too, are absent from this library. Just that one omission alone would make a fairly good library out of a library that hadn't a book in it.

*Mark Twain (1835–1910), on Jane Austen (1775–1817)*

A large shaggy dog just unchained scouring the beaches of the world and baying at the moon.

*Robert Louis Stevenson (1850–94), on Walt Whitman (1819–91)*

The death of a member of the lower classes could be trusted to give him a good chuckle.

*W. Somerset Maugham (1874–1965), on Henry James (1843–1916)*

A cliché-ridden humbug and pie-fingering hack.

*Dylan Thomas (1914–53), on Richard Church (1893–1972), author*

I cannot abide Conrad's souvenir shop style and bottled ships and shell necklaces of romanticist clichés.

*Vladimir Nabokov (1899–1977), on Joseph Conrad (1857–1924)*

Chaucer, notwithstanding the praises bestowed upon him, I think obscene and contemptible; he owes his celebrity merely to his antiquity.

*Lord Byron (1788–1824), on Geoffrey Chaucer (c. 1345–1400)*

A huge pendulum attached to a small clock.

*Ivan Panin, Russian critic, on Samuel Taylor Coleridge (1772–1834), poet*

The undisputed fame enjoyed by Shakespeare as a writer . . . is, like every other lie, a great evil.

*Leo Tolstoy (1828–1910), on William Shakespeare (1564–1616)*

Why sir, Sherry is dull, naturally dull; but it must have taken him a great deal of pains to become what we now see him. Such excess of stupidity, sir, is not in nature.

*Samuel Johnson (1709–84), on Thomas Sheridan (1719–88), Irish actor, elocutionist, and author*

I am fairly unrepentant about her poetry. I really think that three quarters of it is gibberish. However, I must crush down these thoughts, otherwise the dove of peace will shit on me.

*Noël Coward (1899–1973), on Dame Edith Sitwell (1887–1964)*

A poor creature, who has said or done nothing worth a serious man taking the trouble of remembering.

*Thomas Carlyle (1795–1881), on Percy Bysshe Shelley (1792–1822)*

To see him fumbling with our rich and delicate English is like seeing a Sèvres vase in the hands of a chimpanzee.

*Evelyn Waugh (1903–66), on Stephen Spender (1909–95)*

Dean Swift, by his lordship's own account, was so intoxicated with the love of flattery, he sought it amongst the lowest of people and the silliest of women; and was never so well pleased with any companions as those that worshiped him, while he insulted them.

*Lady Mary Wortley Montagu (1689–1762), on Jonathan Swift (1667–1745)*

Conrad spent a day finding the *mot juste*: then killed it.

*Ford Madox Ford (1873–1939), on Joseph Conrad (1857–1924)*

Not quite Milton, a sort of origami Milton, the paper phoenix fluttering in the wizard's hand.

*Hugh Kenner, on Wallace Stevens (1879–1955), American poet*

Jo Davies goes wobbling with his arse out behind as though he were about to make everyone he meets a wall to piss against.

*John Manningham, English diarist, on Sir John Davies (1569–1626), English poet and attorney general*

To the King's theatre, where we saw *A Midsummer Night's Dream*, which I had never seen before, nor shall ever again, for it is the most insipid, ridiculous play that I ever saw in my life.

*Samuel Pepys (1633–1703), English diarist, on a play by William Shakespeare (1564–1616)*

The first man to have cut a swathe through the theater and left it strewn with virgins.

*Frank Harris (1856–1931), English author and journalist, on George Bernard Shaw (1856–1950)*

He seems to me the most vulgar-minded genius that ever produced a great effect in literature.

*George Eliot (1819–80), British novelist, on Lord Byron (1788–1824)*

Gertrude Stein's prose is a cold, black suet-pudding. We can represent it as a cold suet-roll of fabulously reptilian length. Cut it at any point, it is . . . the same heavy, sticky, opaque mass all through, and all along.

*Wyndham Lewis (1882–1957), British painter and author, on Gertrude Stein (1874–1946)*

I loathe you. You revolt me stewing in your consumption . . . the Italians were quite right to have nothing to do with you. You are a loathsome reptile—I hope you die.

*D. H. Lawrence (1885–1930), to Katherine Mansfield (1888–1923), New Zealand–born British author*

He had not the intellectual equipment of a supreme modern poet; except for his genius he was an ordinary nineteenth-century gentleman, with little culture and no ideas.

*Matthew Arnold (1822–88), British poet and critic, on Lord Byron (1788–1824)*

A coxcomb who would have gone into hysterics if a tailor had laughed at him.

*Ebenezer Elliott (1781–1849), British poet and steel founder, on Lord Byron*

Mad, bad, and dangerous to know.

*Lady Caroline Lamb (1785–1828), British aristocrat and writer, on Lord Byron*

The world is rid of Lord Byron, but the deadly slime of his touch still remains.

*John Constable (1776–1837), British artist, upon Lord Byron's death*

The most affected of sensualists and the most pretentious of profligates.

*Algernon Charles Swinburne (1837–1909), poet, on Lord Byron*

The language of Aristophanes reeks of his miserable quackery: it is made up of the lowest and most miserable puns; he doesn't even please the people, and to men of judgment and honor he is intolerable; his arrogance is insufferable, and all honest men detest his malice.

*Plutarch (c. 46–c. 120), Greek biographer and moralist, on Aristophanes (c. 448–c. 388 B.C.), Greek playwright*

Poor Matt. He's gone to heaven, no doubt, but he won't like God.

*Robert Louis Stevenson (1850–94), on Matthew Arnold (1822–88), British poet and critic*

Freud Madox Fraud.

*Osbert Sitwell (1892–1969), British writer, on Ford Madox Ford (1873–1939), British writer*

E. M. Forster never gets any further than warming the teapot. He's a rare fine hand at that. Feel this teapot. Is it not beautifully warm? Yes, but there ain't going to be no tea.

*Katherine Mansfield (1888–1923), in her* Journal *(1917), on E. M. Forster (1879–1970), British novelist*

He is a mediocre man—and knows it, or suspects it, which is worse; he will come to no good, and in the meantime he's treated rudely by waiters and is not really admired even by the middle-class dowagers.

*Lytton Strachey (1880–1932), British writer, on E. M. Forster*

He is limp and milder than the breath of a cow.

*Virginia Woolf (1882–1941), on E. M. Forster*

Of Byron one can say, as of no other English poet of his eminence, that he added nothing to the language, that he discovered nothing in the sounds, and developed nothing in the meaning, of individual words.

*T. S. Eliot (1888–1965), on Lord Byron (1788–1824)*

This awful Whitman. This postmortem poet. This poet with the private soul leaking out of him all the time. All his privacy leaking out in a sort of dribble, oozing into the universe.

*D. H. Lawrence (1885–1930), on Walt Whitman (1819–91), American poet*

Some call Pope little nightingale—all sound and no sense.

*Lady Mary Wortley Montagu (1689–1762), English writer, on Alexander Pope (1688–1744)*

Monsieur Zola is determined to show that if he has not genius he can at least be dull.

*Oscar Wilde (1854–1900), on Émile Zola (1840–1902), French novelist*

The jingle man.

*Ralph Waldo Emerson (1803–82), on Edgar Allan Poe (1809–49)*

I invariably miss most of the lines in the last act of an Ibsen play; I always have my fingers in my ears, waiting for the loud report that means that the heroine has just Passed On.

*Dorothy Parker (1893–1967), on Henrik Ibsen (1828–1906)*

[He is] bent on groping for horror by night, and blinking like a stupid old owl when the warm sunlight of the best of life dances into his wrinkled eyes.

The Gentlewoman *magazine, on Henrik Ibsen*

Henry James had turned his back on one of the great events in the world's history, the rise of the United States, in order to report tittle-tattle at tea parties in English country houses.

*W. Somerset Maugham (1874–1965), on Henry James*

I detest the country. Yeats will amuse me part of the time and bore me to death with psychical research the rest. I regard the visit as a duty to posterity.

*Ezra Pound (1885–1972), American poet, on visiting William Butler Yeats (1865–1939), Irish poet*

[A book by Henry James] is like a church lit but without a congregation to distract you, with every light and line focused on the high altar. And on the altar, very reverently placed, intensely there, is a dead kitten, an eggshell, a bit of string.

*H. G. Wells (1866–1946), on Henry James (1843–1916)*

. . . [S]tewed-up fragments of quotation in the sauce of a would-be dirty mind.

*D. H. Lawrence (1885–1930), on James Joyce (1882–1941)*

I don't think I have ever seen a nastier-looking man. Some people show evil as a great racehorse shows breeding. They have the dignity of a hard chancre. Lewis did not show evil; he just looked nasty.

*Ernest Hemingway (1899–1961), on Wyndham Lewis (1882–1957)*

Byron can only bore the spleen.

*Charles Lamb (1775–1834), on Lord Byron*

He is blatant, full of foolish archaisms, obscure through awkward language, not subtle thought, and formless.

*Rupert Brooke (1887–1915), on Ezra Pound (1885–1972)*

I believe he creates a milieu in which art is impossible.

*Ezra Pound, on G. K. Chesterton (1874–1936)*

Nothing but a pack of lies.

*Damon Runyon (1884–1946), on* Alice in Wonderland *by Lewis Carroll (1832–98)*

From the moment I picked up your book until I laid it down I was convulsed with laughter. Someday I intend reading it.

*Groucho Marx (1895–1977), on* Dawn Ginsbergh's Revenge *by Sydney J. Perelman*

I fell asleep reading a dull book, and I dreamed that I was reading on, so I awoke from sheer boredom.

*Heinrich Heine (1797–1856)*

A Methodist parson in Bedlam.

*Horace Walpole (1717–97), on Dante (1265–1321)*

Here are Johnny Keats's piss-a-bed poetry, and three novels by God knows whom. . . . No more Keats, I entreat: flay him alive; if some of you don't I must skin him myself: there is no bearing the driveling idiotism of the Mankin.

*Lord Byron (1788–1824), on John Keats (1795–1821)*

The kind of man that Keats was gets ever more horrible to me. Force of hunger for pleasure of every kind, and want of all other force—such a soul, it would once have been very evident, was a chosen vessel of Hell.

*Thomas Carlyle (1795–1881), on John Keats*

Byron!—he would be all forgotten today if he had lived to be a florid old gentleman with iron-gray whiskers, writing very long, very able letters to *The Times* about the repeal of corn laws.

*Max Beerbohm (1872–1956), on Lord Byron (1788–1824)*

An unmanly sort of man whose love life seems to have been largely confined to crying in laps and playing mouse.

*W. H. Auden (1907–73), on Edgar Allan Poe (1809–49)*

Of all bitches alive or dead, a scribbling woman is the most canine.

*Lord Byron, on Anna Seward (1747–1809), British poet*

Walt Whitman is as unacquainted with art as a hog with mathematics.

London Critic, *on Walt Whitman (1819–91)*

Longfellow is to poetry what the barrel-organ is to music.

*Van Wyck Brooks (1886–1963), American critic, on Henry Wadsworth Longfellow (1807–82)*

Waldo is one of those people who would be enormously improved by death.

*Saki, pseudonym of H. H. Munro (1870–1916), on Ralph Waldo Emerson (1803–82)*

Carlyle is a poet to whom nature has denied the faculty of verse.

*Alfred, Lord Tennyson (1809–92), on Thomas Carlyle (1795–1881)*

We can say of Shakespeare, that never has a man turned so little knowledge to such great account.

*T. S. Eliot (1888–1965), on William Shakespeare (1564–1616)*

I have tried lately to read Shakespeare, and found it so intolerably dull that it nauseated me.

*Charles Darwin (1809–82), on William Shakespeare*

A strange horrible business, but I suppose good enough for Shakespeare's day.

*Queen Victoria (1819–1901), on Shakespeare's* King Lear

It is not surprising to learn that Marlowe was stabbed in a tavern brawl: what would be utterly unbelievable would be his having succeeded in stabbing anyone else.

*George Bernard Shaw, on Christopher Marlowe (1564–93)*

George too Shaw to be Good.

*Dylan Thomas (1914–53), on George Bernard Shaw (1856–1950)*

Poor Shelley always was, and is, a kind of ghastly object; colorless, pallid, tuneless, without health or warmth or vigor.

*Thomas Carlyle (1795–1881), on Percy Bysshe Shelley (1792–1822)*

I really enjoy his stage directions. . . . He uses the English language like a truncheon.

*Max Beerbohm (1872–1956), on George Bernard Shaw*

Mr. Shaw is (I suspect) the only man on earth who has never written poetry.

*G. K. Chesterton (1874–1936), on George Bernard Shaw*

Then Edith Sitwell appeared, her nose longer than an anteater's, and read some of her absurd stuff.

*Lytton Strachey (1880–1932), on Dame Edith Sitwell (1887–1964)*

Isn't she a poisonous thing of a woman, lying, concealing, flipping, plagiarizing, misquoting, and being as clever a crooked literary publicist as ever.

*Dylan Thomas (1914–53), on Dame Edith Sitwell*

Steele might become a reasonably good writer if he would pay a little attention to grammar, learn something about the propriety and disposition of words, and, incidentally, get some information on the subject he intends to handle.

*Jonathan Swift (1667–1745), on Richard Steele (1672–1729)*

. . . [A] perpetual functioning of genius without truth, feeling, or any adequate matter to be functioning on.

*Gerard Manley Hopkins (1844–89), on Algernon Swinburne (1837–1909)*

Let simple Wordsworth chime his childish verse, and brother Coleridge lull the babe at nurse.

*Lord Byron (1788–1824)*

Everything which another man would have hidden, everything the publication of which would have made another man hang himself, was a matter of exaltation to his weak and diseased mind.

*Thomas Babington Macaulay (1800–59), British historian, on James Boswell (1740–95), author and biographer*

A vain silly, transparent coxcomb without either solid talents or a solid nature.

*J. G. Lockhart (1794–1854), Scottish writer, on Samuel Pepys (1633–1703), diarist*

A good man fallen among Fabians.

*Attributed to Vladimir Ilyich Lenin (1870–1924), on George Bernard Shaw (1856–1950)*

He walked as if he had fouled his small clothes and looks as if he smelt it.

*Christopher Smart (1722–71), British poet, on Thomas Gray (1716–71), British poet*

You can gain nothing by reading her. It is like eating snowballs, with which one can surfeit one's self without satisfying the stomach.

*Napoléon Bonaparte (1769–1821), on Madame Marie de Sévigné (1626–96), French epistolary writer*

There is no arguing with Johnson; for when his pistol misses fire, he knocks you down with the butt end of it.

*Oliver Goldsmith (1728–74), British poet, on Samuel Johnson (1709–84)*

A great author, notwithstanding his *Dictionary* is imperfect, his *Rambler* pompous, his *Idler* inane, his *Lives* unjust, his poetry inconsiderable, his learning common, his ideas vulgar, his *Irene* a child of mediocrity, his genius and wit moderate, his precepts wordy, his politics narrow, and his religion bigoted.

*Robert Potter, British critic, on Samuel Johnson, in 1781*

In George Meredith there is nothing but crackjaw sentences, empty and unpleasant in the mouth as sterile nuts.

*George Moore (1852–1933), on George Meredith (1828–1909)*

I should never write on him as I detest him too much ever to trust myself as a critic of him.

*Ezra Pound (1885–1972), on George Meredith*

Vain Nashe, railing Nashe, cracking Nashe, bibbing Nashe, swaddish Nashe, roguish Nashe . . . the swish-swash of the press, the bum of impudency, the shambles of beastliness.

*Gabriel Harvey (c. 1550–1631), scholar and writer, on Thomas Nashe (1567–1601), English playwright*

This dodipoule, this didopper. . . . Why, thou arrant butter whore, thou cotqueane & scrattop of scoldes, with thou never leave afflicting a dead Carcasse . . . a wispe, a wispe, rippe, rippe, you kitchin-stuff wrangler!

*Thomas Nashe, on Gabriel Harvey*

Dear Sam,
I shall take your advice and not read your book. It would probably pain me and not benefit you.
Your Affectionate father,
T. Butler

*Canon T. Butler to his son, Samuel Butler (1835–1902)*

It is long, yet vigorous, like the penis of a jackass.

*Sydney Smith (1771–1845), British clergyman, wit, and essayist, on the writings of Henry Peter Brougham (1778–1868), British statesman*

Dank, limber verses, stuft with lakeside sedges, And propt with rotten stakes from rotten hedges.

*Walter Savage Landor (1775–1864), British poet, on William Wordsworth (1770–1850), British poet*

Mr. Wordsworth, a stupid man, with a decided gift for portraying nature in vignettes, never ruined anyone's morals, unless, perhaps, he has driven some susceptible persons to crime in a very fury of boredom.

*Ezra Pound (1885–1972), on William Wordsworth*

A blatant Bassarid of Boston, a rampant Maenad of Massachusetts.

*Algernon Charles Swinburne (1837–1909), British poet, on Harriet Beecher Stowe (1811–96), American humanitarian and novelist*

Open him at any page: and there lies the English language not, as George Moore said of Pater, in a glass coffin, but in a large, sultry, and unhygienic box.

*Dylan Thomas (1914–53), on William Wordsworth (1770–1850)*

Anyone who has seen Saint-Marc Giradin walking the street has been immediately struck by the notion of a big goose, deeply in love with itself, but scuttling over the road in panic to escape from a coach.

*Charles Baudelaire (1821–67), on Saint-Marc Giradin, an anti-Romantic critic and publicist*

Our authors are vulgar, gross, illiberal; the theater swarms with wretched translations and ballad operas and we have nothing new but improving abuse.

*Horace Walpole (1717–97), British author, on his life and time*

Tennyson is a beautiful half of a poet.

*Ralph Waldo Emerson (1803–82), on Alfred, Lord Tennyson (1809–92)*

There was little about melancholy that he didn't know; there was little else that he did.

*W. H. Auden (1907–73), on Alfred, Lord Tennyson*

I don't think Robert Browning was very good in bed. His wife probably didn't care for him very much. He snored and had fantasies about twelve-year-old girls.

*W. H. Auden, on Robert Browning (1812–89)*

The way Bernard Shaw believes in himself is very refreshing in these atheistic days when so many people believe in no God at all.

*Israel Zangwill (1864–1926), British dramatist and novelist, on George Bernard Shaw (1856–1950)*

In his endeavors to corrupt my mind he has sought to make me smile first at Vice, saying, "There is nothing to which a woman may not be reconciled by repetition or familiarity." There is no vice with which he has not endeavored in this manner to familiarize me.

*Annabella Milbanke, Lady Byron, on her husband, Lord Byron (1788–1824)*

He has never been known to use a word that might send a man to a dictionary.

*William Faulkner (1897–1962), on Ernest Hemingway (1899–1961)*

Poor Faulkner. Does he really think emotions come from big words?

*Ernest Hemingway, on William Faulkner*

He is a system of assumed personas.

*H. G. Wells (1866–1946), on Ford Madox Ford (1873–1939)*

A nice, acrid, savage, pathetic old chap.

*I. A. Richards (1893–1979), English literary critic, on Robert Frost (1874–1963)*

The work of Henry James has always seemed divisible by a simple dynastic arrangement into three reigns: James I, James II, and the Old Pretender.

*Philip Guedalla (1889–1944), British historian and biographer, on Henry James (1843–1916)*

I have just read a long novel by Henry James. Much of it made me think of the priest condemned for a long space to confess nuns.

*William Butler Yeats (1865–1939), on Henry James*

I could not write the words Mr. Joyce uses: my prudish hands would refuse to form the letters.

*George Bernard Shaw (1856–1950), on James Joyce (1882–1941)*

My God, what a clumsy olla putrida James Joyce is! Nothing but old fags and cabbage stumps of quotations from the Bible and the rest stewed in the juice of deliberate, journalistic dirty-mindedness.

*D. H. Lawrence (1885–1930), on James Joyce*

Probably Joyce thinks that because he prints all the dirty little words he is a great hero.

*George Moore (1852–1933), on James Joyce*

Kipling is a jingo imperialist, he is morally insensitive and aesthetically disgusting.

*George Orwell (1903–50), on Rudyard Kipling (1865–1936)*

A mercenary, hypochondriacal flibbertigibbet who doesn't take in one of six words addressed to him.

*Evelyn Waugh (1903–66), British novelist, on Beverly Nichols, British writer*

His very frankness is a falsity. In fact, it seems falser than his insincerity.

*Katherine Mansfield (1888–1923), on her husband, John Middleton Murry (1889–1957)*

He would not blow his nose without moralizing on the conditions in the handkerchief industry.

*Cyril Connolly (1903–74), on George Orwell (1903–50)*

The Hitler of the book racket.

*Wyndham Lewis (1884–1957), on Arnold Bennett (1867–1931)*

I don't regard Brecht as a man of iron-gray purpose and intellect. I think he is a theatrical whore of the first quality.

*Peter Hall (b. 1930), British director, on Bertolt Brecht (1898–1956)*

Cibber! write all thy Verses upon Glasses,
The only way to save them from our Arses.

*Alexander Pope (1688–1744), on Colley Cibber (1671–1757)*

In an old writer, and especially one of that age, I never saw so large a proportion of what truly be called either trash or ordure.

*Robert Southey (1774–1843), British poet laureate, on Robert Herrick (1591–1684), English poet*

Never did I see such apparatus got ready for thinking, and never so little thought. He mounts scaffolding, pulleys, and tackles, gathers all the tools in the neighborhood with labor, with noise, demonstration, precept, and sets—three bricks.

*Thomas Carlyle (1795–1881), on Samuel Taylor Coleridge (1772–1834)*

He keeps one eye on a daffodil and the other on a canal share.

*Walter Savage Landor (1775–1864), on William Wordsworth (1770–1850)*

It is written by a man with a diseased mind and soul so black that he would even obscure the darkness of hell.

*Senator Reed Smoot, on* Ulysses *by James Joyce (1882–1941)*

His brain is a half-inch layer of champagne poured over a bucket of Methodist near-beer.

*Benjamin de Casseres (1873–1945), American journalist and author, on George Bernard Shaw (1856–1950), Irish-English playwright and socialist agitator*

He is a shallow, affected, self-conscious fribble.

*Vita Sackville-West (1892–1962), on Max Beerbohm (1872–1939)*

Ben Jonson! Not another word about him. It makes my blood boil! I haven't the patience to hear the fellow's name. A pigmy! An upstart! A presumptuous valet who dared to be thought more of than Shakespeare in his day!

*Walter Savage Landor (1775–1864), poet and essayist, on Ben Jonson (1576–1637), poet and playwright*

Oscar Wilde's talent seems to me to be essentially rootless, something growing in glass on a little water.

*George Moore (1852–1933), Anglo-Irish novelist, on Oscar Wilde (1854–1900)*

The great honor of that boast is such
That hornets and mad dogs may boast as much.

*Lord Hervey (1696–1743), on Alexander Pope (1688–1744)*

Byron dealt chiefly in felt and furbelow, wavy Damascus daggers, and pocket pistols studded with paste.

*Walter Savage Landor (1775–1864), poet and essayist, on Lord Byron (1788–1824)*

. . . [T]he poetry has a good deal of staple about it, and will bear handling; but the inner, the conversational and private, has many coarse intractable dangling threads, fit only for the flockbed equipage of grooms.

*Walter Savage Landor, on William Wordsworth (1770–1850)*

I forgive your reviling of me: there's a shovelful of live coals for your head—does it burn? And am, with true affection—does it burn now?
Ever yours,
Charles Dickens

*Charles Dickens (1812–70), in a letter to Walter Savage Landor*

Master, mammoth, mumbler.

*Robert Lowell (1917–77), American poet, on Ford Madox Ford (1873–1939)*

The languid way in which he gives you a handful of numb unresponsive fingers . . .

*Thomas Carlyle (1795–1881), on William Wordsworth (1770–1850)*

[He looks like] an umbrella left behind at a picnic.

*George Moore (1852–1933), on W. B. Yeats (1865–1939)*

. . . [A] charlatan, a fool, a lunatic or a child.

*R. D. Blumenfield, editor of the* Daily Express, *on Sir Arthur Conan Doyle (1859–1930)*

It is a better thing to be a starved apothecary than a starved poet. So back to the shop, Mr. John. Back to plaster, pills, and ointment boxes.

*J. G. Lockhart in* Blackwood's Magazine *(1818), on John Keats*

Sir Walter Scott, when all is said and done, is an inspired Butler.

*William Hazlitt (1778–1830), on Sir Walter Scott (1771–1832)*

A desiccated bourgeois . . . a fossilized chauvinist, a self-satisfied Englishman.

Pravda, *on George Bernard Shaw (1856–1950)*

Trollope! Did anyone bear a name that predicted a style more Trollopy?

*George Moore (1852–1933), on Anthony Trollope (1815–82)*

That insolent little ruffian, that crapulous lout. When he quitted a sofa, he left behind him a smear. My wife says he even tried to paw her about.

*Norman Cameron (1905–53), British poet, on Dylan Thomas (1914–53)*

What a tiresome, affected sod.

*Noël Coward (1899–1973), on Oscar Wilde (1854–1900)*

Lawrence is in a long line of people, beginning with Heraclitus and ending with Hitler, whose ruling motive is hatred derived from megalomania, and I am sorry to see that I was once so far out in estimating him.

*Bertrand Russell (1872–1970), on D. H. Lawrence (1885–1930)*

With leering Looks, Bull-fac'd and frekl'd fair,
With two left legs, and Judas colour'd Hair,
And frowzy Pores that taint the ambient Air.

*John Dryden (1631–1700), on Jacob Tonson, a publisher*

A louse in the locks of literature.

*Alfred, Lord Tennyson (1809–1892), on Churton Collins, a critic*

The verses, when they were written, resembled nothing so much as spoonfuls of boiling oil, ladled out by a fiendish monkey at an upstairs window upon such of the passers-by whom the wretch had a grudge against.

*Lytton Strachey (1880–1932), on the poetry of Alexander Pope (1688–1744)*

Yet let me flap this bug with gilded wings,
This painted child of dirt, that stinks and sings . . .

*Alexander Pope (1688–1744), on John Hervey, Baron Hervey of Ickworth (1696–1743), British courtier and writer*

. . . [A] poor, thin, spasmodic hectic shrill and pallid being.

*Thomas Carlyle (1795–1881), on Percy Bysshe Shelley (1792–1822)*

Wordsworth has left a bad impression wherever he visited in town by his egotism, vanity, and bigotry.

*John Keats (1795–1821), on William Wordsworth (1770–1850)*

A mere ulcer; a sore from head to foot; a poor devil so completely flayed that there is not a square inch of healthy flesh on his carcass; an overgrown pimple, sore to the touch.

Quarterly Review, *in 1817, on William Hazlitt (1778–1830)*

Emerson is one who lives instinctively on ambrosia—and leaves everything indigestible on his plate.

*Friedrich Wilhelm Nietszche (1844–1900), on Ralph Waldo Emerson (1803–82)*

He is a sort of Marquis de Sade, but does not write so well.

*Edmund Gosse (1849–1928), on James Joyce (1882–1941)*

Just for a handful of silver he left us,
Just for a riband to stick in his coat.

*Robert Browning (1812–1889), on William Wordsworth (1770–1850)*

Stoeber's mind, though that is no name to call it by . . . turns as unansweringly to the false, the meaningless, the unmetrical, as the needle to the pole.

*A. E. Housman (1859–1936), British poet and classicist, on Elias Stoeber (1719–78), editor of classical texts*

What does pain me exceedingly is that you should write so badly. These verses are execrable, and I am shocked that you seem unable to perceive it.

*Edmund Gosse, (1849–1928), British poet and literary critic, to Robert Nichols (1893–1944), British poet and dramatist*

Our language sunk under him.

*Joseph Addison (1672–1719), on John Milton (1608–74)*

*Paradise Lost* is one of the books which the reader admires and lays down, and forgets to take up again. Its perusal is a duty rather than a pleasure.

*Samuel Johnson (1709–84), on Milton's* Paradise Lost

This obscure, eccentric, and disgusting poem.

*Voltaire (1694–1778), on* Paradise Lost *by John Milton*

About as credulous as an old goose as one could hope to find out of Gotham.

*B. G. Johns, in* John Aubrey of Wilts, *on John Aubrey (1626–97), English biographer and antiquarian*

You talk about yourself a great deal. That's why there are no distinctive characters in your writing. Your characters are all alike. You probably don't understand women; you've never depicted one successfully.

*Leo Tolstoy (1828–1910), to Maxim Gorky (1868–1936)*

Fielding had as much humor perhaps as Addison, but, having no idea of grace, is perpetually disgusting.

*Horace Walpole (1717–97), on Henry Fielding (1707–54)*

If you imagine a Scotch commercial traveler in a Scotch commercial hotel leaning on the bar and calling the barmaid Dearie, then you will know the keynote of Burns's verse.

*A. E. Housman (1859–1936), on Robert Burns (1759–96)*

I attempt to describe Mr. Swinburne; and lo! the Bacchanal screams, the sterile Dolores sweats, serpents dance, men and women wrench, wriggle and foam in an endless alliteration of heated and meaningless words.

*Robert Buchanan (1841–1901), on Algernon Charles Swinburne (1837–1909)*

She is stupid, heavy, and garrulous. Her ideas on morals have the same length of judgment and delicacy of feeling as those of janitresses and kept women . . . she has good reasons to wish to abolish Hell.

*Charles Baudelaire (1821–67), on George Sand (1804–76)*

# 9
# ON PHILOSOPHERS, ANALYSTS, GOD, AND THE DEVIL

What a hideous, odd-looking man Sydney Smith is!
With a mouth like an oyster, and three double chins.

*Mrs. Brookfield, on Sydney Smith (1771–1845)*

Smug Sydney.

*Lord Byron (1788–1824), on Sydney Smith*

I must believe in the Apostolic Succession, there being no other way of accounting for the descent of the Bishop of Exeter from Judas Iscariot.

*Sydney Smith (1771–1845), British clergyman, writer, and wit, on the Bishop of Exeter*

The truth is that Sydney Smith is naturally coarse, and a lover of scurrilous language.

*John Ward, Earl of Dudley (1781–1833), on Sydney Smith*

My prayer to God is a very short one: "Oh, Lord, make my enemies ridiculous." God has granted it.

*Voltaire (1694–1778)*

God is the only being who, in order to rule, does not need even to exist.

*Charles Baudelaire (1821–67)*

You get the impression this is another dirty wop, an organ grinder.

*W. H. Auden (1908–73), on Pope Pius XII (1875–1958)*

Hume's philosophy, whether true or false, represents the bankruptcy of eighteenth-century reasonableness.

*Bertrand Russell (1872–1970), British philosopher, on David Hume (1711–76), Scottish philosopher*

The next time anyone asks you "What is Bertrand Russell's Philosophy?," the correct answer is "What year please?"

*Sydney Hook, on Bertrand Russell*

Luther was the foulest of monsters.

*Pope Gregory XV (1554–1623), on Martin Luther (1483–1546)*

The Lord strike him with madness and blindness. May the heavens empty upon him thunderbolts and the wrath of the Omnipotent burn itself unto him in the present and future world. May the Universe light against him and the earth open to swallow him up.

*Pope Clement VI (1478–1534), on a now-anonymous subject*

He stood on the flat road to heaven and buttered slides to hell for all the rest.

*Oliver Wendell Holmes (1841–1935), on George Santayana (1863–1952), American philosopher*

Voltaire, or the anti-poet—the king of nincompoops, the prince of the superficial, the anti-artist, the spokesman of janitresses.

*Charles Baudelaire (1821–67), on Voltaire (1694–1778)*

A liar and a father of lies.

*Dante (1265–1321), on the devil*

A philosophizing serpent.

*Horace Walpole (1717–97), British letterist and memoirist, on Mary Wollstonecraft (1759–97), British feminist*

She is an infidel . . . a vulgar and foolish one.

*John Ruskin (1819–1900), British art critic and author, on Harriet Martineau (1802–76), British feminist, philanthropist, and writer*

Against Locke's philosophy I think it an unanswerable objection that, although he carried his throat about with him in this world for seventy-two years, no man ever condescended to cut it.

> *Thomas de Quincey (1785–1859), British writer, in "On Murder Considered as One of the Fine Arts" (1827), on John Locke (1632–1704), English philosopher*

Actually I always loathed the Viennese quack. I used to stalk him down dark alleys of thought, and now we shall never forget the sight of old, flustered Freud seeking to unlock his door with the point of his umbrella.

> *Vladimir Nabokov (1899–1977), on Sigmund Freud (1856–1939)*

The bear loves, licks, and forms her young, but bears are not philosophers.

> *Edmund Burke (1729–97), on Jean-Jacques Rousseau (1712–78)*

. . . [O]ne of the most depraved, vicious and revolting humbugs who ever escaped from a nightmare or a lunatic asylum.

*Preston Sturges (1898–1959), American film director, on Aleister Crowley (1875–1947), British poet*

The arch-Philistine Jeremy Bentham was the insipid, pedantic, leather-tongued oracle of the bourgeois intelligence of the nineteenth century.

*Karl Marx (1818–83), German political philosopher, on Jeremy Bentham (1748–1832), British political philosopher*

Maybe it would have been better if neither of us had been born.

*Napoléon Bonaparte (1769–1821), on Jean-Jacques Rousseau (1712–78)*

The Puritan hated bear-baiting, not because it gave pain to the bear, but because it gave pleasure to the spectators.

*Thomas Babington Macaulay (1800–59), in his* History of England

Plato is a bore.

*Friedrich Wilhelm Nietzsche (1844–1900)*

If God were suddenly condemned to live the life which he has inflicted on men, he would kill himself.

*Alexandre Dumas fils (1824–95)*

Man is quite insane. He wouldn't know how to create a maggot, and he creates Gods by the dozen.

*Michel de Montaigne (1533–92)*

No one ever made more trouble than "Gentle Jesus, meek and mild."

*James M. Gillis, (1811–1865), American naval officer and astronomer, on Jesus*

A parish Demagogue.

*Percy Bysshe Shelley (1792–1822), on Jesus*

Susan is lean, cadaverous, and intellectual, with the proportions of a file and the voice of a hurdy-gurdy.

*Anonymous writer in the* New York World *(1866), on Susan B. Anthony (1820–1906), American feminist*

I have no patience whatever with these Gorilla damnifications of humanity.

*Thomas Carlyle (1795–1881), on Charles Darwin (1809–82)*

# 10
# ON THE STAGE

---

A crazy fanatic . . . a crazy cranky being . . . not only consistently dirty, but deplorably dull. . . . A gloomy sort of ghoul . . . blinking like a stupid old owl.

*Newspaper review of* Hedda Gabler *by Henrik Ibsen (1828–1906)*

An ego like a raging tooth.

*W. B. Yeats (1865–1939), on Mrs. Patrick Campbell (1865–1940), actress*

Superabundance of foulness . . . wholly immoral and degenerate . . . you cannot have a clean pig sty.

*Newspaper review of* Mrs. Warren's Profession *by George Bernard Shaw (1856–1950)*

Smells to high heaven. It is a dramatized stench.

*Newspaper review of* Mrs. Warren's Profession

Two things should be cut—the second act and the child's throat.

*Noël Coward (1899–1973), on a dull play with an annoying child star*

. . . [H]is figure is that of a hippopotamus, his face like the bull and mouth on the panels of a heavy coach, his arms are fins flattened out of shape, his voice the gargling of an alderman with the quinsy, and his acting altogether ought to be a natural, for it is certainly like nothing that Art has ever exhibited on stage.

*Lord Byron (1788–1824), on Master William Betty (1791–1874), child actor*

A woman whose face looked as if it had been made of sugar and someone had licked it.

*George Bernard Shaw (1856–1950), on Isadora Duncan (1878–1927), American dancer*

To me Edith looks like something that would eat its young.

*Dorothy Parker (1893–1967), on Dame Edith Evans (1888–1976), British actress*

My Dear Sir,
I have read your play.
Oh, my dear Sir.
Yours Faithfully

*Henry Beerbohm Tree (1853–1917), to a would-be dramatist*

Foote is quite impartial, for he tells lies of everybody.

*Samuel Johnson (1709–84), on Samuel Foote (1720–77), British actor and dramatist*

The ideal of the haberdashery clerk and of all the other chumps who had never heard of Rubens or the Greeks or fresh air.

*Ralph Barton, on Lillian Gish (1896–1993), American actress*

He will ultimately take his stand in the social rank . . . among the swindlers, blacklegs, pickpockets, and thimble-riggers of his day.

> *Anonymous writer, in* Tait's Edinburgh Magazine *(1855), on Phineas Taylor Barnum (1810–91), American showman*

She was so dramatic she stabbed the potatoes at dinner.

> *Sydney Smith (1771–1845), on Mrs. Sarah Siddons (1755–1831), English actress*

# 11 ON MEN, WOMEN, LOVE, AND MARRIAGE

---

I could do without your face, Chloe, and without your neck, and your hands, and your limbs, and to save myself the trouble of mentioning the points in detail, I could do without you altogether.

*Martial (c. 40–104), Roman poet*

Love is the affection of a mind that has nothing better to engage it.

*Theophrastus (c. 372–287 B.C.), Greek philosopher*

A word to you of Lady Caroline Lamb. I speak from experience—keep clear of her (I do not mean as a woman that is all fair). She is a villainous intriguante in every sense of the word, mad and malignant, capable of all and every mischief. Above all, guard your connections from her society. With all her apparent absurdity, there is an indefatigable and active spirit of meanness and destruction about her which delights and often succeeds in inflicting misery.

*Lord Byron (1788–1824), in a letter to James Wedderburn Webster*

Love may arise from a generous sentiment—namely, the liking for prostitution; but it soon becomes corrupted by the liking for ownership.

*Charles Baudelaire (1821–67), French poet*

Woman is the opposite of the Dandy. That is why she should be regarded with disgust . . . woman is "natural"—that is to say, abominable. Moreover she is always vulgar—that is to say the opposite of the Dandy.

*Charles Baudelaire*

I have always been amazed that women are allowed to enter churches. What sort of conversations can they have with God?

*Charles Baudelaire*

There is only one way to be happy by means of the heart—to have none.

*Paul Bourget, French psychologist, in 1890*

Lord, she is Thin.

*Annapolis County grave epitaph*

Love, in present-day society, is just the exchange of two momentary desires and the contact of two skins.

*Nicholas Chamfort, French aphorist, in 1805*

Man remains what he has always been; the cruelest of all the animals, and the most elaborately and fiendishly sensual.

*George Bernard Shaw (1856–1950), on men*

She was never really charming until she died.

*Terence (c. 185–159 B.C.), epitaph to an unknown woman*

Oh love will make a dog howl in tune.

*Francis Beaumont and John Fletcher, playwrights, in 1608*

Brigands demand your money or your life. Women demand both.

*Attributed to Samuel Butler (1612–80)*

. . . [F]or although women might make excellent bookkeepers, there is much in accountancy proper that is, we think, unsuitable for them.

*English Institute of Chartered Accountants, in* The Accountant *(1912)*

The more I see of men, the more I admire dogs.

*Marie de Rabutin-Chantal, Marquise de Sévigné (1626–96)*

A woman is only a woman,
But a good cigar is a smoke.

*Rudyard Kipling (1865–1936); later used by Groucho Marx (1895–1977)*

The five worst infirmities that afflict the female are indocility, discontent, slander, jealousy, and silliness.

*Confucian marriage manual*

The Queen is most anxious to enlist every one who can speak or write to join in checking this mad wicked folly of "Woman's Rights" with all its attendant horrors, on which her poor feeble sex is bent, forgetting every sense of womanly feeling and propriety.

*Queen Victoria (1819–1901)*

There is but one thing in the world worse than a shameless woman, and that's another woman.

*Aristophanes (c. 448–380 B.C.), in* Thesmophoriazusae

Such is the human race. Often it does seem a pity that Noah and his party didn't miss the boat.

*Mark Twain (1835–1910)*

If you pick up a starving dog and make him prosperous, he will not bite you. That is the principal difference between a dog and a man.

*Mark Twain*

A man is in general better pleased when he has a good dinner upon his table, than when his wife talks Greek.

*Samuel Johnson (1709–1840)*

The male is by nature superior, and the female inferior: the one rules and the other is ruled.

*Aristotle (384–322 B.C.), in* Politics

Too often the strong silent man is silent because he does not know what to say, and is reputed strong only because he has remained silent.

*Winston Churchill (1874–1965)*

Man originates in muck, wades a while in muck, makes muck and in the end returns to muck.

*Johann Christoff Friedrich von Schiller (1759–1805), German playwright, in* The Robbers *(1781)*

I sometimes think that God, in creating man, somewhat overestimated his ability.

*Oscar Wilde (1854–1900)*

It is only the man whose intellect is clouded by his sexual impulses that could give the name of "the fair sex" to that undersized, narrow-shouldered, broad-hipped and short-legged race.

*Arthur Schopenhauer (1788–1860), German philosopher*

Once a woman has given you her heart you can never get rid of the rest of her body.

*John Vanbrugh (1664–1726), British playwright, in* The Relapse *(1696)*

The history of women is the history of the worst tyranny the world has ever known: the tyranny of the weak over the strong. It is the only tyranny that ever lasts.

*Oscar Wilde (1854–1900)*

Their slanderous tongues are so short, and the time wherein they have lavished out their words freely hath been so long, that they know we cannot catch hold of them to pull them out, and they think we will not write to reprove their lying lips.

*Jane Anger, in* Protection for Women *(1589), on men*

A "Grand Old Man." That means on our continent anyone with snow-white hair who has kept out of jail until eighty.

*Stephen Leacock, English-born Canadian humorist, in 1910*

God created Adam, lord of all living creatures, but Eve spoiled it all.

*Martin Luther (1483–1546)*

I consider that women who are authors, lawyers, and politicians are monsters.

*Auguste Renoir (1840–1919)*

The dissoluteness of our lascivious, impudent rattle-pated gadding females is now such . . . they are lowde and stubborne; their feet abide not in their houses; now they are without, now in the streets, and lie in wait in every corner; being never well pleased nor contented, but when they are wandering abroad to Playes, the Playhouses, Dancing-Matches, Masques and publick Shewes.

*William Prynne (1600–69), English pamphleteer*

Twenty million young women rose to their feet with the cry "We will not be dictated to" and promptly became stenographers.

*G. K. Chesterton (1874–1936)*

Mrs. Balinger is one of those ladies who pursue Culture in bands, as though it were dangerous to meet it alone.

*Edith Wharton (1862–1937), American novelist*

It was very good of God to let Carlyle and Mrs. Carlyle marry one another and so make only two people miserable instead of four.

*Samuel Butler (1835–1902), on Thomas Carlyle (1795–1881)*

The majority of husbands remind me of an orangutan trying to play the violin.

*Honoré de Balzac (1799–1850)*

Marriage—a friendship recognized by the police.

*Robert Louis Stevenson (1850–94)*

The music at a wedding procession always reminds me of the music of soldiers going into battle.

*Heinrich Heine (1797–1856)*

Unfaithful bitch! Messalina! Medusa! Gorgon!

*Roman Emperor Claudius (10 B.C.–A.D. 54), on Valeria Messalina, his wife*

She was a prymerole, a piggensye,
For any Lord to leggen in his bedde.
Or yet for any good yeman to wedde.

*Geoffrey Chaucer (c. 1343–1400), English poet*

I bequeath all my property to my wife on the condition that she remarry immediately. Then there will be at least one man to regret my death.

*Heinrich Heine (1797–1856), German poet and critic*

Here lies my wife.
Here let her lie!
Now she's at rest,
And so am I.

*John Dryden (1631–1700), English poet (proposed)*
*"Epitaph for His Wife"*

Marriage is a desperate thing. The frogs in Aesop were extreme wise; they had a great mind to some water, but they would not leap into the well, because they could not get out again.

*John Selden, English historian, in* Table Talk *(1689)*

If you're afraid of loneliness, don't marry.

*Anton Chekhov (1860–1904)*

It is embarrassing how he harps on his wife's dimensions: brave little heart, noble little creature, indomitable little soul—he only just stops short of "wee cowering crimson-tippit Beastie."

*Sylvia Townsend Warner (1893–1978), British reteller of the classics, on Thomas Carlyle (1795–1881)*

You might people a colony with her; or give an assembly with her; or perhaps take your morning walks around her, always providing there were frequent resting places and you are in rude health. I was once rash enough to try walking around her before breakfast, but only got half way and gave up exhausted. Or you might read the Riot Act and disperse her; in short, you might do anything with her but marry her.

*Sydney Smith (1771–1845), British clergyman, writer, and wit, on the news that an acquaintance was to marry a very overweight woman*

# 12
# ON ONESELF

---

How unpleasant to meet Mr. Eliot!
With his features of clerical cut,
And his brow so grim
And his mouth so prim
And his conversation, so nicely
Restricted to What Precisely
And If and Perhaps and But.

*T. S. Eliot (1888–1965), on himself, in "Five Finger Exercises"*

When I don't look like the tragic muse, I look like the smoky relic of the great Boston Fire.

*Louisa May Alcott (1832–88), on herself*

He was meddling too much in my private life.

*Tennessee Williams (1911–83), on why he had stopped visiting his psychoanalyst*

I became one of the stately homos of England.

*Quentin Crisp, writer and actor*

You have but two topics, yourself and me, and I'm sick of both.

*Samuel Johnson (1709–84), on James Boswell (1740–95), British author and biographer*

I think I may boast myself to be, with all possible vanity, the most unlearned and uninformed female who ever dared to be an authoress.

*Jane Austen (1775–1817), on herself, to the Reverend James Clarke*

If people only knew as much about painting as I do, they would never buy my pictures.

*Sir Edwin Henry Landseer (1802–73), to W. P. Frith, British artist*

My handwriting looks as if a swarm of ants, escaping from an ink bottle, had walked over a sheet of paper without wiping their legs.

*Sydney Smith (1771–1845)*

Somebody's boring me. I think it's me.

*Dylan Thomas (1914–53)*

# INDEX

Page numbers in plain text indicate pages with insulting remarks made by the subject; those in bold indicate pages with insulting remarks made to or on the subject. Italicized page numbers indicate pages with both insulting remarks made on the subject and others made by the subject.